Stepping-Stones to Further Jewish–Lutheran Relationships

Key Lutheran Statements

Edited by Harold H. Ditmanson

Published in cooperation with
the Ditmanson Endowment Fund
of St. Olaf College

Augsburg ■ Minneapolis

STEPPING-STONES TO FURTHER JEWISH–LUTHERAN RELATIONSHIPS
Key Lutheran Statements

Scripture quotations unless otherwise noted are from the Revised Standard Version of the Bible, copyright © 1946, 1952, and 1971 by the Division of Christian Education of the National Council of Churches.

Cover design: Mark Stratman

Library of Congress Cataloging-in-Publication Data

Stepping-stones to further Jewish–Lutheran relationships : key
    Lutheran statements / edited by Harold H. Ditmanson.
       p.   cm.
    "Published in cooperation with the Ditmanson Endowment Fund of St.
Olaf College."
    Includes bibliographical references.
    ISBN 0-8066-2461-2
    1. Judaism—Relations—Lutheran Church—Sources. 2. Lutheran
Church—Relations—Judaism—Sources. 3. Judaism (Christian
theology)—History of doctrines—Sources. I. Ditmanson, Harold H.
BM535.S6925   1990
261.2'6—dc20   89-29903
                                           CIP

The paper used in this publication meets the minimum requirements of American National Standard for Information Sciences—Permanence of Paper for Printed Library Materials, ANSI Z329.48-1984. ∞™

Manufactured in the U.S.A.   AF 9-2461

94   93   92   91   90   1   2   3   4   5   6   7   8   9   10

Contents

3

Contents

Additional Documents

Foreword

I met Harold at a colloquium on Jewish–Lutheran relations. I noticed that he would speak little, but slowly and to the point. At our colloquium he pointed out clearly and strongly the meaningful mission of Israel in God's design. He felt that this recognition is essential in the way Christians relate to Jews on the end of the 20th century. One could feel his commitment, the warmth of his relationship and his deep concern for the prophetic encounter of Christians and Jews despite history.

Harold was especially aware of the Christian accusation that the Jewish people were a deicide community. He considered this matter central in a Christian reckoning of the soul in order to understand the Sinai Covenant of God with Israel. In the introduction of the present volume, he stressed that the denial of the deicide charge leads straight to the conclusion that Judaism has a reality and autonomy of its own and a positive place in the divine economy. The rejection of the deicide charge stands at one end of the line, but the affirmation of Judaism's covenant and integrity stands at the other end of that line. Harold could not see how a thoughtful Christian could fail to move on to that point after having affirmed the first point.

Harold had read and studied much about Jewish history prior to 1964, but that year he received an invitation that changed his life. His response when the Jewish Community Relations Council presented him with the first Jewish–Christian Relations Award in 1987 tells the story:

> The knowledge I had gained from newspapers, journals, and books about the sufferings of Jewish people through the centuries and more recently in Nazi Germany remained in my mind to afflict me. But there was relatively little I could do about it apart from putting it to use as I taught my courses in biblical

studies, church history, ethics, and systematic theology. There was no ecclesiastical vehicle or commission to do anything with this knowledge about the Jewish people, their religion and their history. The situation changed drastically and made my knowledge existential and urgent when Dr. Arne Sovik, a staff member of the Lutheran World Federation, invited me to represent my church at the Løgumkloster consultation. I received from his office a big packet of study materials. As I read the papers about Jewish history, Jewish worship, Jewish biblical interpretation, Christian anti-Semitism, the Nazi Holocaust, and the other topics, I found myself in a new world of information and imperatives. As an educated person, much of this knowledge was familiar to me, but there was no department or commission to fashion a program that would do something with the knowledge. Then, in 1964, there was a responsibility laid directly upon me, and some new organizations were created to carry out what needed to be done.

From that time on, Harold was committed to advancing Jewish–Christian relations, speaking out on behalf of mutual respect and understanding between Christianity and Judaism. His pioneering leadership heralded a new era in Christian attitudes toward Jews, and he played a key role in writing and editing many of the statements in this book.

Harold understood *meeting* as an encounter in God, facing each other as partners in God's design, being called by God to be in conversation, using verbs and nouns with diverse nuances and words to express commitments that are different but equal in their translation of God's summons. For Harold, God was found in the face of the other in encounter and dialogue.

That is exactly the meaning of the interfaith encounter with Harold: to be with him was to share in silence and words the Presence of God because of Harold's presence as a person of God. Our friendship developed slowly, meaningfully, and became essential. To relate to him was an encounter of faith, respectful of different commitments but attentive to God and to our duty to witness as friends a covenantal relationship in the world.

Harold was a person who needed other people. He needed the biblical "face to face" encounter in order to deepen his own commitment and his belief in our meeting of hearts and souls. I remember at our interreligious meetings we would take a walk, or sit by a window facing the trees, sharing a cup of coffee. We commented on theological matters, on the direction that the interreligious dialogue was taking. We also were silent. We needed silence to cement points of the discussion. But we essentially required silence to work amongst each other in our spiritualities, in our being in God, to be together in reflection and hope.

Harold did not accept individualism. He was committed to personal relationships. He believed in a personalism that took into account God's creation of the human being as a unique contribution to redemption. The personal relationship was a process of being with other persons, bringing together the Kingdom delayed by alienation and spiritual arrogance.

He felt it a moral imperative to establish a relationship with Judaism, to understand Jewish commitment, spiritual aims, and the Jewish vocation to serve humanity and God. This moral imperative was central in his consideration of anti-Semitism in all its forms, from post-Lutheran rabid anti-Jewish feelings to present anti-Zionist stands. Harold recognized Judaism and his Jewish friends as partners in God's design, as witnessing together at a time of trouble and confusion.

His dream was to see Christians and Jews together in a dialogue of equals, subjects of faith, a faith that recognized God as the unique source of meaning and spiritual salvation. He worked for that all his life.

Harold was an example for all of us. We share his feeling as presented in his conclusion:

> The thesis that has gradually taken shape during my 20 years of involvement in Jewish–Lutheran relations is that full recognition of the reality of Judaism as a living religion is the essential precondition for any biblically sound, theologically coherent, and humanly fruitful contact between Judaism and Christianity in the future. . . . If the Jews are not the object of a special form of divine punishment, then there is no reason that God has abandoned them or cancelled his covenant with them—the form such punishment would take. But if God has not abandoned the Jews, then he must still be with them, in which case their survival, including the practice of their religion, must be due not to God's anger or their own blindness but to God's gracious, providential design. If this is the case, then Judaism must have a genuine basis of its own in its ongoing covenantal relationship with God. In short, aJudaism has a witness God wants it to bear.

Harold's voice, commitment, and deep spirituality still sound in these words. Harold was a presence, sharing his spiritual presence with people, always in the Presence of God. We, his friends, are grateful to God for this gift.

RABBI LEON KLENICKI, Director
Department of Interfaith Affairs
Anti-Defamation League of B'nai B'rith

Publisher's Note

Harold H. Ditmanson, a pioneering leader in the field of Jewish–Christian relationships, was born September 23, 1920, in New Richmond, Wisconsin. He received his B.A. from St. Olaf College, Northfield, Minnesota, additional degrees from Luther Theological Seminary and Princeton Theological Seminary, and a Ph.D. from Yale University. He taught at Augsburg College, Waldorf Junior College, and then St. Olaf from 1945 to his retirement in 1985.

He married Jean Hanson in 1943. Their four children are Barbara, Mary, Anne, and Mark.

Dr. Ditmanson became a member of the Lutheran World Federation's Committee on the Church and the Jews in 1964, and in 1969 he was appointed to the Commission on the Church and the Jewish People of the World Council of Churches. In 1975 he was named to serve on the Standing Committee of Lutheran-Jewish Concerns of the American Lutheran Church. He wrote numerous articles on Jewish–Christian relations for both Christian and Jewish journals.

In 1987 he was chosen to receive the first Jewish–Christian Relations Award from the Jewish Community Relations Council for his groundbreaking work and years of dedicated leadership.

In 1988, Dr. Ditmanson died after a long illness. Both Christians and Jews thank God for the life of Harold Ditmanson, a bearer of light and a witness to God's love.

The Lutheran Statements

Introduction by
Harold H. Ditmanson

Harold Ditmanson presented the following address in New York City at a 1983 fact-finding conference, "Luther and the Jews," cosponsored by the Lutheran Council in the USA and the American Jewish Committee.

In this address, he gave an overview of Jewish–Christian relations and then summarized the first nine statements printed in this book. The overview is reprinted here as the introduction to part 1; the summaries, however, now serve as introductions to the statements.

THE UNEASY TENSION

A few years ago, Dr. Seymour Siegel wrote some words that have been a source of great encouragement to many Christians. In the Winter/Spring 1976 issue of *Face to Face* he said: "There is a new appreciation of Judaism in Christian circles. The history and theology of Jewish religion is being taught sympathetically in Christian schools. The deicide charge has been repudiated in both Catholic and Protestant churches. There are numerous meetings and conferences all over the world where individuals professing different religions can discuss their fears and hopes. Here and there vestiges of the old enmity persist. But clearly the direction is towards mutuality and dialogue."

This is a generous and hopeful comment. I believe it is an accurate one. Christians have made positive moves towards Judaism and their Jewish neighbors during the past 20 years. The consciences of Christians could not allow them to forget or ignore the fate of the Jewish people during the

11

era of the holocaust. In a confused, inadequate—yet genuine—way Christians have asked to be forgiven for their part in the centuries of defamation and mistreatment of the Jewish people. They have especially wanted to respond in a spirit of repentance and cooperation to the calamities of the twentieth century. Sensitive Christians in positions of leadership have pledged themselves to the prevention of such tragedies in the future.

The year 1983 marks the 500th anniversary of Martin Luther's birth. A veritable flood of literature has appeared in which every aspect of Luther's life and work has been reexamined. The evaluation of Luther's anti-Semitic writings is of special interest to us. It must be acknowledged that Luther was not, however, the creator or even the most extreme representative of anti-Semitic attitudes. All Christians have been involved in anti-Jewish attitudes and actions since the second century, and Luther was a part of this negative tradition.

From our standpoint, we criticize Luther for not rising above the conventional theology and prejudice of his time. He was an original thinker in many respects, but not in all respects. Because of the undue and unhealthy prominence given Luther by later generations, his late negativism toward Jews was exploited. It is important, of course, to see Luther in the context of the period from 1523 to 1543 and to trace through the next four centuries the degree of his influence as regards anti-Semitism. To see Luther in his context is not an attempt to excuse him or to excuse any other Lutherans at any other time. The desperate facts about what Christians, including Lutherans, have said and done are clear. We have to admit that they are there, acknowledge that Jews have ample reason for resentment and fear, and pledge to do everything within our power to eliminate this dreadful part of the Christian tradition.

Both Lutherans and Jews agree that more fact finding is needed. In view of Luther's prominence among so many Protestant Christians, what do we in fact have to deal with? We are looking at a broadly based, ancient Christian negativism towards Judaism and Jewish people. Luther was a part of this tradition. The facts indicate that he failed to reject an inhumane tradition. The failure of others was greater and more damaging. By seeing Luther in context, we have not excused him but have underscored the magnitude of the problem. We Lutherans acknowledge our corporate involvement in this tragic history. There is little gain in fixing sole or major responsibility upon Luther. That oversimplifies the problem. The facts regarding the publication and use of his anti-Semitic writings over 400 years tell one story: The main stream of Lutheranism was embarrassed by or ignorant of Luther's anti-Semitic writings, but did accept his exclusively Christological interpretation of the Hebrew Scriptures, and the notion that the church had replaced Israel. These factors helped create a climate within which an essentially pagan hatred of Jews, as Raul Hilberg puts it, could take root and flourish.

Lutherans today have decisively rejected Luther's anti-Jewish prejudice and are in the process of dealing with the traditional theology of rejection and substitution, which can generate feelings of superiority and even hostility toward Jews. The difficult task of reconsidering the traditional theology of replacement must be carried forward because we have come to recognize the unstable character of a position that is limited to or aims primarily at the goal of defusing anti-Semitism and treating Jewish neighbors with respect and justice. There is an uneasy tension between the policy of treating Jewish people with respect on a moral basis and the policy of regarding Judaism as a defective and replaceable religion from a theological point of view. There are many Christians who believe that unless we clarify in a new and decisive way the theological premises of our approach to Judaism, we cannot expect to move forward to a stage of real meeting and mutual enrichment, nor can we anticipate that within the foreseeable future we will see an end of anti-Jewish attitudes.

The situation among Christians at the present time, to judge by their public statements, is one in which all agree about the moral or humanitarian dimension of Jewish–Christian relations. It is necessary to make amends for past wrongs and to cooperate with all citizens of good will in guaranteeing security and justice for our Jewish neighbors now and in the future. But beyond this point Christians are divided. Some say that the moral commitment can operate on its own level and coexist with a theology of replacement issuing in a program of mission and conversion. Still other Christians insist that the moral and theological levels are in fact interrelated and that the church must take some new steps in clarifying its "theology of Israel." This is necessary, they say, because Christianity has not displaced Israel as the people of God and because the moral commitment is not safe so long as a theology of rejection and substitution gives support to the notion that Judaism is not a living religion, a true covenant between God and his people. A traditional view endorses the moral commitment and combines it with a theology of replacement and a program of mission. A revisionist view endorses the moral commitment and combines it with a theology of recognition and a program of dialogue, of mutual listening and receiving.

The Christian statements that have been issued during the past 20 years have been drafted by representative groups. These groups have not all been of one mind. In fact, some members themselves have not been all of one mind! The split between traditionalist and revisionist view has run not only between individuals but within individuals, resulting in the not uncommon spectacle of a mind divided against itself. Therefore almost all recent Christian declarations about Judaism and Christianity are marked by the tension between moral and theological components, and between traditional and revisionist theological perspectives. The Jewish–Christian encounter has at long last entered a new stage of movement, for which we can be profoundly grateful, but the Christian community is of a divided mind about it.

Lutheran statements appearing between 1964 and 1982 exhibit the mixture of positions I have just described. There are nine such statements that I wish to analyze:

- "The Church and the Jewish People," the Løgumkloster report of the Lutheran World Federation, parts I–III, 1964, and part IV, 1969;
- "The Church and the Jewish People," the Neuendettelsau report of the Lutheran World Federation, 1973;
- "The Oneness of God and the Uniqueness of Christ: Christian Witness and the Jewish People," the Oslo report of the Lutheran World Federation, 1975;
- "Some Observations and Guidelines for Conversations between Lutherans and Jews," Lutheran Council in the USA, 1971;
- "The American Lutheran Church and the Jewish Community," The American Lutheran Church, 1974;
- "To Share Gospel with Jews," Lutheran Church–Missouri Synod, 1977;
- "To Encourage Evangelism among the Jews," Lutheran Church–Missouri Synod, 1977;
- "A Statement of Jewish-Lutheran Concerns," Lutheran Church–Missouri Synod, 1978;
- "The Significance of Judaism for the Life and Mission of the Church," the Bossey report of the Lutheran World Federation, 1982.

Several of the Lutheran participants in this conference ["Luther and the Jews," October, 1983, New York City] have had a hand in drafting, publicizing, and implementing these statements. My colleagues at this consultation, as well as others, may or may not agree with my interpretation of these Lutheran statements. Our collective memories do, however, constitute an important part of the living archives of recent Lutheran concern and activity with respect to Judaism, and it may be helpful if I record even briefly my understanding of what we have tried to accomplish.

The assignment to examine several documents is very inclusive and elastic. It allows the examiner great freedom of approach. Since there is no authorized model of analysis, I am going to provide a simple conceptual instrument for the process of examination. I suggest that we track throughout these documents a threefold mixture of elements: (1) a moral imperative, (2) a traditionalist theological perspective, and (3) a revisionist theological perspective. These components are present in all the statements, though in different proportions, with different degrees of emphasis, and with different relationships to each other.

Earlier Catholic and Protestant Declarations

As a background to our examination of Lutheran statements, let me refer briefly to earlier Protestant and Catholic declarations in order to show that the divided mind of Christianity is a general and not just a Lutheran phenomenon.

In 1948 the First Assembly of the World Council of Churches produced a statement that included the three elements I have designated. On the moral level it condemned anti-Semitism and acknowledged the guilt of the churches. On the level of traditional theological affirmation it urged the evangelization of the Jews, apparently on the ground that Christianity had replaced Judaism in the scheme of salvation. It was said, however, that this mission should be carried on as a normal part of parish outreach rather than by special agencies. On the level of what might have been a revisionist theological accent, it acknowledged Israel's place in God's design. I say this *might* have been a new or nontraditional accent because such statements about "Israel's place in God's design" are nearly always ambiguous, and in 1948, the WCC statement described this special place as a *mystery*.

In 1954, the Second Assembly of the World Council of Churches again asserted on the moral level that Christians have been guilty of anti-Semitism. This admission was combined with the theological claim that the church cannot rest until its Jewish brethren have accepted Christ as Savior.

In 1961 the Third Assembly of the World Council of Churches condemned anti-Semitism and specifically rejected the deicide charge. Christians were further urged, on the moral level, to fight against all forms of discrimination. On the theological level it was said that Jews must find God in Christ, but alongside this traditional claim one found an affirmation of the primacy of God's election of the Jews. This latter statement is left so inexact that it is not clear whether it is a new and revisionist accent or not. Other WCC documents place theologies of rejection and of recognition side by side, thus testifying to the compromising character of such statements.

A 1964 resolution of the National Council of Churches in the USA confessed that Christians have misrepresented the New Testament story of the death of Christ and have also in other ways been guilty of anti-Semitism. The common spiritual heritage of Jews and Christians was recognized and interfaith dialogue and common service to humankind were urged. Here again one finds a blend of the moral and the theological elements, but with the traditional mission idea given little prominence.

In 1965 the Second Vatican Council issued its historic declaration on the "Relation of the Church to the Non-Christian Religions." On the moral level anti-Semitism was explicitly denounced, along with the associated themes of deicide and deserved suffering. The traditional theological claim was made that the church should hope and work for the conversion of Jews to Christianity. But some new or revisionist accents were sounded when the declaration affirmed the indissoluble tie between Israel and the church, and said that God had *not* withdrawn his presence from Jewish faith and worship.

This is very significant in view of the historic Christian notion that Jewish religion, after the redemption accomplished by Christ, fell into a state of blindness and consequently the worship taking place in synagogues was not the adoration of the true God, but was empty and hollow because the God of the covenant was no longer there. The Vatican statement clearly says that Jewish religion has a positive place in God's plan for universal salvation.

The Vatican declaration included another significantly new theme. It said that although the church is the new people of God, the Jews should not be presented as rejected or accursed by God, "*as if* this followed from the Holy Scriptures." Centuries of Christian exegesis had simply assumed from the reading of a familiar set of New Testament texts that Jewish religion had been rejected by God. The Vatican statement opened the way for exegetes to look at the apparently anti-Jewish New Testament sayings in a broader context which would transcend the theory of rejection and substitution.

It is my impression that once the doors had been opened by Vatican II, the Catholic church, at many levels and in several countries, moved resolutely and effectively toward a clarification of its "theology of Israel." As one reads the official Catholic documents issued between 1965 and 1975, as one examines Eugene Fisher's excellent book, *Faith Without Prejudice*, and his many articles, and as one studies addresses given recently by Pope John Paul II and by other officials of the church, notably Archbishop John Roach of Minnesota, it seems very clear that a dividing line between past and present has been drawn in the Catholic tradition. The movement definitely leans away from the traditional theology of supersession and towards a full acknowledgment of the continuing reality of the Jewish covenant with God and the continuing role of that people of God on its own terms.

There are many Protestant statements in which Methodists, Episcopalians, Baptists, Presbyterians, and others have taken what is for them the big step of affirming the permanent election of the Jewish people as the people of God and asserting that through Jesus Christ the church is taken into the covenant of God with his people. Most of these declarations include the three elements I have mentioned: the moral imperative, the traditional call to evangelize everyone, and a revisionist affirmation of the continuing reality of Judaism.

Against this background we can turn to an examination of Lutheran statements which have appeared during the period from 1964 to 1982. These Lutheran statements are, as we have seen, part of a general movement among Christians. This movement is characterized by a greater awareness of Christian responsibility for Jewish suffering, a growing determination to make amends for the past and to safeguard the future security of Jewish people, and an increasing uneasiness about the ambiguity of the traditional "theology of Israel." Lutherans share in this climate of thought and feeling. The several statements are not peculiarly "Lutheran," with the exception of references to the role Luther played in the phenomenon of anti-Semitism. These statements are not distinctive but they do represent what Lutherans in all their variety have thought and felt and said from within their own faith tradition.

1

The Church and
the Jewish People

"The Løgumkloster Report"

INTRODUCTION BY HAROLD H. DITMANSON

The first official Lutheran declaration, the Løgumkloster report, was produced in 1964, although there had been Lutheran participation in earlier ecumenical statements and individuals, churches, and groups had spoken out within the Lutheran family prior to that time. The Lutheran World Federation's Department of World Mission called a "Consultation on the Church and the Jewish People" at Løgumkloster, Denmark, April 26 to May 2, 1964. The meeting was attended by about 40 persons from 14 countries. Among them were theologians, pastors, missionaries, several Christians of Jewish background, representatives of the Commission of the Church and the Jewish People of the World Council of Churches, and Rabbi Arthur Gilbert of the National Conference of Christians and Jews. No participant can ever forget the admirable manner in which Rabbi Gilbert represented the Jewish people. In some important sense he served as the conscience of the consultation.

Bishop Heinrich Meyer of Lubeck presided and stated the reasons for calling a representative assembly of Lutherans. He pointed out that the relationship of the Christian church to the Jewish people had always been a very special problem because of their common faith in the God of Abraham, Isaac, and Jacob, yet their divergence at the point of faith in Jesus of Nazareth as the Messiah. But the historic problems of interrelationship and opposition have been accentuated, Bishop Meyer said, by two modern developments. First, "the outbreak of murderous anti-Semitism in recent history and the persistence of anti-Semitism in many parts of the world." Second, "the Christian church is in a process of reconsidering and reinterpreting its mission." Bishop Meyer had himself been a missionary and a mission executive. This reconsideration inevitably raised the question about missions to the Jewish people. Should there be a special mission to the Jews, distinct from the mission to other non-Christians? If so, what would be its unique features? The assembly was divided into several task forces, each assigned to draft a statement on a specific topic. During the last three days the drafts were discussed and revised and the first three sections were accepted. They appear in the report as "The Church and Israel," "Mission and Dialog," and "The Church and Anti-Semitism." The task force which attempted to draw up a statement on the "theological appraisal of the relationship of the church and the Jewish People" was unable to present a draft to the plenary session which could be accepted. This particular group included representatives of widely different perspectives on mission or, to put it another way, on the theological meaning of Israel's continuing existence. As we have already seen, this has always been the point of ambiguity, the point at which the special relationship between Israel and the church has been asserted but not defined.

It was in this group that Lutherans faced most sharply the tension between the traditional and the revisionist theological elements. Two strong personalities represented two "theologies of Israel." Professor Karl Heinrich Rengstorff, a man of great learning, prestige, and personal force, expressed the traditional view that the "old" Jewish order or covenant has given way to a "new" Christian covenant, and that Christianity has succeeded to the spiritual position of Judaism. Even though the draft of this group was not completed, Professor Rengstorff's influence and point of view are expressed in sections I and II of the final report, which relate mission to the Jews to the incompleteness of Jewish religion.

Opposing Professor Rengstorff and the majority of the assembly was the perspective of Professor Gunther Harder of Berlin. Professor Harder contended that Christians should urge Jews to remain Jews and to stand in the place where God's wisdom and patience had placed them. "There can be no missionary intention on the Christian side in the Christian–Jewish conversation. It will always be the case for the Christian that he sees the Jew oriented toward and dependent upon God's gracious future. As to the way in which men will reach that future, the Christian will leave to the counsel of God." Professor Harder's view found no place in the report and he refused to associate himself with most of the document.

Bishop Meyer noted that the report of the consultation would have to be left unfinished due to "certain differences of opinion" about the church's theology of Israel and urged that the work of the consultation be continued. Consequently the Commission on World Mission of the Lutheran World Federation recommended the appointment of a special committee which would follow up on the work of the consultation and would have the particular task of writing a statement on "the theology of the church's relation to Judaism." The committee was made up of twelve persons, eight representatives of churches, and four staff members. Professor Rengstorff was a member. There were three from North America—George Forell, Arne Siirala, and Harold Ditmanson. Arne Sovik, Martin Kretzmann, and Paul Hoffman participated as staff members. Others represented Germany, Finland, Sweden, and Denmark. The committee discussed many topics and drafted many papers over a period of five years. Eventually it completed a statement in 1969 which became section IV of the final report. The completed document was submitted to the Commission on World Mission that same year.

The passage of time, the composition of the committee, and the experiences the group went through from 1964 to 1969 all had an effect on the content of section IV. Section IV, with Professor Rengstorff's consent, went beyond what had been said before by any Lutheran group. There was in fact a rather obvious tension between sections I and II and section IV. In the interests of tidiness let me comment first on section III of the Løgumkloster document, for it is in that section that the *moral component* makes its appearance. In drafting that chapter I had the assistance of Dr. A. Roy Eckhardt, who was present as an observer.

The six members of the drafting group represented Lutheran churches in the United States, Canada, Germany, Holland, and Finland. Early one morning we began our consideration of what the Lutheran churches ought to say about anti-Semitism. One member of the committee had been a young soldier in an American army unit that opened the gates of a death camp shortly after the flight of its German army guards. His subsequent life and thought had been radically affected by the horror of what he saw there.

Another member of the committee was a Dutch pastor who carried vivid memories of the Dutch resistance movement and of such incidents as the fate of Anne Frank and her family. A German committee member was the senior pastor of a large urban parish. He had seen the rise and fall of the entire Nazi movement and was still hearing in the voices of fellow Lutherans echoes of Nazi anti-Semitism. Each member of the committee had his own agenda, rooted in personal observations of the consequences of anti-Semitism.

As the discussion proceeded that morning, it seemed clear to me that no single scheme of interpretation, suitable for a draft statement, would emerge from our general conversation. About 10:00 A.M. I suggested that each member of the committee retire to his room and spend the time until 4:00 P.M. writing out his own version of what ought to be said. We reconvened in the afternoon and read our statements to each other. Roy Eckhardt was not only a careful student of anti-Semitism, but was also a seasoned veteran of many Methodist assemblies in which he had served on drafting committees. I co-opted his services and together Dr. Eckhardt and I worked until far into the night composing a unified statement. I presented this draft to the committee the next morning. The committee accepted the statement although one member complained that the only part of his draft that he could recognize was the word *God*.

This statement on anti-Semitism was accepted enthusiastically and without revision by the entire assembly. This was no doubt due to the fact that the text did express the deep feelings and convictions of everyone present. There was no divided mind on the level of moral obligation. The statement did not touch on ambiguous theological topics and Lutherans who could not agree on "the theology of Israel" could speak with one voice about the moral imperative.

The historic accusations of deicide and rejection are explicitly repudiated. The guilt of Christian people is confessed. The sentence "as Lutherans, we confess our own peculiar guilt," has a special meaning. Most committee members favored a strongly worded sentence which would acknowledge the tragic consequences of Martin Luther's anti-Semitic writings, would declare them to be wrong and indefensible, and would dissociate modern Lutherans from the understanding of church and synagogue which is set forth in Luther's writings on the Jews. A German pastor, however, urged the committee to avoid making such a specific reference to Luther. "I deplore those writings as much as anyone," he said, "But in my parish and many others, there are secular forces which are seeking to destroy the church. They portray Luther as the spiritual ancestor of Hitler. If we now issue a public denunciation of Luther's anti-Semitism, we will be playing into their hands without helping our Jewish neighbors because these forces are also trying to destroy Judaism. This is a painful dilemma. Luther's later views should be denounced, but not at the cost of giving powerful aid to the enemies of both Christians and Jews."

The committee was persuaded that genuine harm would be done in particular situations and areas by an explicit reference to Luther. Yet it was necessary to say something about this unavoidable element in

Christian–Jewish relations. The compromise reached was to use the sentence, "as Lutherans, we confess our own peculiar guilt." It was understood by conference participants that this language was meant to repudiate Luther's anti-Semitic writings. We hoped our Jewish neighbors would understand that we opposed any attempt to base a policy of discrimination upon those fateful and mistaken writings of Luther. Whether our compromise statement served the pastoral interests of various German Lutherans, I am not able to say.

A note of genuine repentance is sounded in section III and practical measures are suggested for overcoming the plague of anti-Semitism. These paragraphs of the report received favorable attention from many sectors of the Jewish community and we had reason to believe that our statements were taken as sincere and constructive. The recommendation that church literature be examined in order to remove anti-Semitic references has paid off in a most gratifying way, as has the suggestion that Lutherans and Jews meet together for the sake of mutual understanding and common efforts on behalf of human rights. We can turn now to the two theological sections of the report. There is a rather obvious tension between sections I and II, written in 1964, and section IV, written in 1969. Sections I and II express the traditional theology of replacement. Section I acknowledges the shared inheritance of Jews and Christians and the gift of God's grace to the people of the original covenant. It then asserts that the old covenant has been replaced by a new covenant with Christians. The church succeeded to the spiritual position and task of Israel which will not inherit the promises of God until it recognizes Jesus as the Messiah. Alongside this claim lies the idea that God continues to be faithful to Israel. This is called a "mystery," but it probably means that while Israel has closed the door on God, God has not closed the door on Israel. The way is open. Meanwhile Judaism has been made theologically superfluous.

Section II presents the classic Christian concept of mission. The first paragraph describes the universal mission which Christians find in the New Testament. The second paragraph applies this notion to the Jewish people and says that the mission should not single out Jews as special targets but should include them in the normal parish outreach. But if Jews cannot be reached in this way, special mission organizations should bring the gospel to them. All this is consistent with the theology of replacement stated in section I.

Section IV, completed five years later, reflects a changed mood and a long period of wrestling with the central question about which there has been so much ambiguity and disagreement. This section begins in a low-key manner and gradually works its way to some surprising conclusions.

The first three paragraphs of section IV warn against triumphalism and against the complacent acceptance of stereotypes and conventional assumptions.

The fourth paragraph begins to break new ground. It recommends that the Lutheran rubric of law and gospel should be reexamined in the light of the possibility that Paul's polemic against law should be understood not as directed against law as such but against a local or sectarian emphasis within Judaism. If when Paul contrasts works and faith or law and gospel he does not identify Judaism as a whole with works, but rather an eccentric emphasis within Judaism, then Christians cannot complacently speak of Judaism as a religion of works and Christianity as a religion of faith. But if Judaism cannot be seen simply as a religion of works-righteousness, then it *can* be seen as an authentic response to God's grace. If that is the case, then Paul does not contrast Judaism and Christianity in the simple terms of right and wrong, old and new, complete and incomplete. And if Paul does not do that, then the church cannot claim his support for its theology of replacement.

In part 2 of section IV, the first two paragraphs are a murky and circuitous way of disturbing the peace of mind of Christians who hold the traditional view in an uncritical manner. The emphasis upon mystery, paradox, and the limits of logic and understanding make the point that no one should think he can derive from the Bible a simple, complete, and neatly packaged understanding of God's self-revelation in the life, death, and resurrection of Jesus. The whole picture of God's power active in gracious and suffering condescension is awesome and incomprehensible and we can only acknowledge the mystery.

One aspect of this mystery is that Christians have salvation only because Jesus was rejected. Does this not suggest that Jesus was rejected as part of God's design and out of faithfulness rather than stubbornness? Granted, this is a speculative point, but it does at least complicate matters.

The last two paragraphs of part 2 of section IV apply the categories of mystery and paradox to eschatology and ecclesiology. Four points are made here. First, it is wrong for the church to regard the Jewish people from a position of superiority. It is said that the early Luther rejected such triumphalism. Second, it is affirmed that the future rests in God's hands. At this point it is possible to make explicit reference to the anti-Semitic writings of Luther and to repudiate them. Luther is said to be wrong, but the bitter pill is sweetened somewhat by explaining the circumstances in which he went astray. Third, it is said that the church must try to grasp the theological meaning of the holocaust. Fourth, the statement affirms the right of the Jews to exist as a community. The context makes it clear that this refers to the state of Israel.

Part 3 of section IV consists of a set of questions and a number of affirmations. The questions go to the heart of the matter: the claim of Judaism to be a living and true, not a dead, empty religion, and the pertinence of this claim to the Christian "theology of Israel." In the face of all the mystery referred to previously, the implication is that a Lutheran can answer these questions with a yes or a no and be within the orbit of legitimate Lutheran diversity. That is, both traditional and revisionist theories must have a place within Lutheranism. Those who hold the theology of replacement cannot say that their opponents have deviated from the true faith. Thus a window is opened.

The affirmations which follow the questions represent something like theological variations on the theme of solidarity, and they have very important hermeneutical implications.

The first paragraph relates the notion of solidarity to the assertion that God has a people, one people, a people whose unity will one day become visible. Thus, Lutherans cannot take over such phrases as "people of God" or "Israel" as though they did not apply equally to Judaism. Both Christianity and Judaism enjoy continuity with the Israel of Abraham, Isaac, and Jacob. The third paragraph says that in view of all this Lutherans cannot in their exegesis and theology apply negative terms to Jews and positive terms to Christians. The fourth paragraph says that the God of the covenant remains faithful to his promise and continues to be the Lord of the Jewish people and the Lord of Christian believers, the Lord of the *one* people of God.

The conclusion again affirms that the church can have no sense of superiority over the Jewish people, but must see them as partners in dialogue within a common history. The church can only proceed in humility, even as it shares with all humanity its faith and hope. But its hope is for the consummation of two covenants in a future which only God can understand and bring to pass.

If this analysis of section IV is reasonably accurate, then it does appear that it contains themes not fully consistent with sections I and II, written five years earlier. Some Lutherans will think that section IV is simply wrong and a piece of bad theology. Others will welcome it. It is, in any case, a serious effort to clarify any ambiguities involved in talk about "God's continuing faithfulness to his people" and "Israel's place in God's design."

Is this theology of the church's relation to Judaism consistent with missions to the Jews? At no point does the document say a clear no, although many individuals infer such an answer from the argument. The document speaks of both mission and dialogue in such a way that some can pursue the one and some the other. But those who do pursue mission cannot do it on the assumption that all Lutherans agree in seeing Judaism as a dead or empty religion which is not in real contact with the one true God and has therefore been replaced by Christianity.

The Løgumkloster document was the first comprehensive Lutheran statement on Jewish–Christian relations. The Løgumkloster consultation remains the most dramatic and important Lutheran meeting in this area of theological and missionary reflection. The report exhibits both the clarity and forthrightness of the moral response to anti-Semitism and the ambiguities of the theological appraisal of Jewish–Christian encounter.

THE CHURCH AND THE JEWISH PEOPLE

Sections I–III of this document were prepared at a Consultation on the Church and the Jews, convened by the Lutheran World Federation's Department of World Mission at Løgumkloster, Denmark, in 1964. Section IV represents subsequent study by a Committee on the Church and the Jews, which completed its work at a meeting in Geneva, Switzerland, in 1969. The document was presented to the meeting of the LWF Commission on World Mission in Asmara, Ethiopia, that same year, and to the Fifth Assembly of the LWF in Evian, France, in July, 1970.

I. The Church and Israel

The church may use the term Israel theologically only in the sense in which it appears in the Scriptures of the Old and New Testaments: in the first instance, as an expression of God's sovereign grace toward Abraham and his descendants, the people of the old covenant, to whom God revealed his will and promised his redemption for the blessing of the nation; in the second place, as an expression for the people of the new covenant made up of Jews and gentiles in which, through the redemption in Jesus Christ, the gentiles become fellow heirs of the promises. Here we take up both the New Testament assertions about the true seed of Abraham and the typological interpretations of Old Testament history as applied to the church.

Thus the church testifies that, by the fulfillment of the promises in Jesus the Messiah and by his acceptance by but a part of the Jews, a division has arisen which has placed the "old" Israel outside the "new." This division will be healed when "all Israel" (Rom. 11:26) recognizes Jesus of Nazareth as its Messiah. Only then will the mystery of the faithfulness of God toward his people be resolved. Those who share in the inheritance must recognize a grateful responsibility for the original heirs. It follows, therefore, that the church will pray for the Jews daily, especially in its Sunday worship.

Those who in faith through baptism have put on Christ Jesus are all Christians, with distinction, whether they have their origin in the people of the old covenant or among the gentiles. Terms such as "Hebrew Christian," and the like, introduce unbiblical divisions into the church.

The gathering of Jews in the land of the patriarchs may in God's redemptive purposes have special importance. We live much too close to this development, however, to make a specific judgment about its religious significance: God's action in history we are unable to discern.

II. Mission and Dialogue

A. The church is called by its Lord to be his body in the world, and to proclaim the mighty works of God to all men (Acts 2:11). Following the call of its Lord, the church has the responsibility of beseeching all men on behalf of Christ to be reconciled to God (2 Cor. 5:20). Because of this responsibility, the church also has the obligation to carry on organized mission activities through which the message of reconciliation is brought to men. As a member of the body of Christ, every Christian also shares in the "sent-ness" of the church. This quality of "being sent" applies in every area of the Christian's relationship to the world, and he will witness with his whole life in testifying to his faith (1 Peter 3:15), in listening to others, in seeking to understand, and in sharing the burdens of his fellowman.

B. The witness to the Jewish people is inherent in the content of the gospel, and in the commission received from Christ, the head of the church. The mission will most effectively reflect the glory of Christ in his gospel when it is pursued in the normal activity of the Christian congregation, which reflects itself in the Christian witness of the individual members. Where Jewish communities in the world cannot normally be reached by Christian congregations, mission organizations must provide for the proclamation of the gospel to these people.

C. It is a Christian responsibility to seek respectfully to understand both the Jewish people and their faith. Therefore responsible conversations between Christians and Jews are to be desired and welcomed. Such conversations presuppose the existence of common ground on which Christians and Jews may meet, as well as points of difference. The conversations may be carried on through organized institutes, or by individuals and groups. The conversations do not assume an equating of the religions, nor do they require that Christians abstain from making their witness as a natural outgrowth of the discussions. Similarly Christians will listen gladly as Jews explain their insights of faith.

III. The Church and Anti-Semitism

Anti-Semitism is an estrangement of man from his fellowmen. As such it stems from human prejudice and is a denial of the dignity and equality of men. But anti-Semitism is primarily a denial of the image of God in the Jews; it represents a demonic form of rebellion against the God of Abraham, Isaac, and Jacob, and a rejection of Jesus the Jew, directed upon his people. "Christian" anti-Semitism is spiritual suicide. This phenomenon presents a unique question to the Christian church, especially in light of the long and terrible history of Christian culpability for anti-Semitism. No Christian can exempt himself from involvement in this guilt. As Lutherans, we confess our own peculiar guilt, and we lament with shame the responsibility which our church and her people bear for this sin. We can only ask God's pardon and that of the Jewish people.

There is no ultimate defeat of anti-Semitism short of a return to the living God in the power of his grace and through the forgiveness of Jesus Christ our Lord. At the same time, we must pledge ourselves to work in concert with others at practical measures for overcoming manifestations of this evil within and without the church and for reconciling Christians with Jews. Toward this end, we urge the Lutheran World Federation and its member churches:

1. To examine their publications for possible anti-Semitic references, and to remove and oppose false generalizations about Jews. Especially reprehensible are the notions that Jews, rather than all mankind, are responsible for the death of Jesus the Christ, and that God has for this reason rejected his covenant people. Such examination and reformation must also be directed to pastoral practice and preaching references. This is our simple duty under the commandment common to Jews and Christians: "Thou shalt not bear false witness against thy neighbor."

2. To oppose and work to prevent all national and international manifestations of anti-Semitism, and in all our work acknowledge our great

debt of gratitude to those Jewish people who have been instruments of the Holy Spirit in giving us the Old and New Testaments and in bringing into the world Jesus Christ our Lord.

3. To call upon our congregations and people to know and to love their Jewish neighbors as themselves; to fight against discrimination or persecution of Jews in their communities; to develop mutual understanding; and to make common cause with the Jewish people in matters of spiritual and social concern, especially in fostering human rights.

IV. On the Theology of the Church's Relation to Judaism

1. We as Christians can only speak of the Jewish people if we say that we are all human beings standing under God's judgment and in need of his forgiveness. We are all men and women before we are Jews and Christians. What we say here in a special way about the Jews must be understood in the light of this assertion.

The relationship between Jews and Christians has been confused through the centuries by two wrong assumptions. The first assumption falsifies the Christian understanding by seeing the Jews of all times as identical with that Jewish group which in the first century rejected Jesus of Nazareth as Messiah. The second falsifies the Jewish understanding by seeing all Christians as in principle involved in the hate and persecution which were inflicted on the Jews by the official church and by nations claiming a Christian tradition. While this committee claims no competence to remove the existing negative opinions held by Jews, it must contribute to the task of eliminating all those barriers raised by past and present Christian misunderstanding which stand in the way of our conversation with the Jews and our understanding of their faith.

We shall have to engage in an ongoing encounter with Jews and Judaism which takes seriously both Jewish and Christian history. In deepening the Jewish–Christian relationship we expect to find ways of understanding each other which have been lost due to historical circumstances. Theological education—and the teaching of church history in particular—will have to undergo considerable revision if this is to be done. Teachers and pastors must be given information and materials so that in their interpreting of biblical texts they will be sensitive to the false assumptions Christians have made.

The distinction between law and gospel which in Lutheran tradition becomes a key for interpreting the whole scriptural revelation is connected with this hermeneutical problem. This specific emphasis places a particular burden on Jewish–Lutheran relations. But for this reason it lends increased urgency to theological encounter. As Lutherans we believe, on the basis of Paul's witness, that it is God's action in Christ which justifies the sinner. Thus we cannot speak about the law and about righteousness as though it were obedience which lays the foundation for relationship to God. The theological issue here touches both Jewish–Christian dialogue and Christian use of the Old Testament. Our understanding can be traced to Luther and his reception through Augustine of certain Pauline motifs. It is possible, however, that our whole outlook has been shaped and a relationship to the Jewish people has been vitiated by a strongly negative understanding of the law and its function. This, it seems to us, might well be a matter for consideration by the Lutheran World Federation Commission on Theology in cooperation with a possible future committee on the church and the Jews.

2. As we try to grasp the theological meaning of the problem we face, we recognize two aspects of the Christian understanding of God's self-disclosure, both of which lead us to the limits of human perception and speech. The first is the fact that with the coming of Jesus into the world a development began which is incomprehensible in its dimensions. It can only be described as an act of God's love for all men. In the moment when according to Christian faith, God acted to bring his revelation to its fulfillment, among those who had first received his revelation many did not find themselves able to respond in faith to what God was now doing in Jesus of Nazareth. In spite of this rejection, however, God's saving grace found a way into the world and no human guilt or rejection could negate it. The faith and the universal proclamation that God became man, that God was in Christ reconciling the world unto himself, that Jesus of Nazareth was the Son of God, is an offense to human wisdom and particularly to the religious view of God's glory. It is as if God had of necessity to meet rejection and to suffer the consequences of his love in order to bring life and salvation to mankind.

The second aspect is closely related to the first. Because Jesus took upon himself his cross and became obedient unto death, God raised him from the dead. His death and resurrection constitute a special Christian hope for the whole world. This implies the crucial paradox that for the Christian faith there is a divine future for mankind since Jesus the Nazarene was rejected. Thus we are here directed toward the mystery of God's inscrutable ways with men.

Mystery and paradox—the point where human logic leads no farther—stand at the center of all Christian thought. That is the case with Christology, but it is equally true of eschatology, and it applies to ecclesiology as well.

God has not only prepared a future for all mankind, but has bound this future to the cross and resurrection of the man Jesus of Nazareth. It is our conviction that the central position of the cross and resurrection of Jesus has fundamental consequences for the understanding of the church. This was perceived and expressed in a unique way by Luther. He did not accept identification of the elect people of God with a specific ecclesiological tradition. This view has led to the fatal alternatives of medieval church-centered theology, in which the Jewish people were treated from a position of superiority. Luther opposed any kind of a "theology of glory," i.e., any attempt to see and proclaim God and his deeds and works (including the church) primarily in terms of might, of lordship, of victory and triumph. The theological paradox which confronted Luther in his historical situation, however, proved to be too much for him. This one can see from his later writings against the Jews. In these polemic tracts a theology of glory does break in. Luther's anxiety about the church's existence became so strong that he found himself no longer able to let the future rest in God's hands but, in anticipation of what he read to be God's future judgment, called upon the secular arm to effect that judgment in the present. In doing so he overstepped the bounds of what it lies in human authority to do, to say nothing of love. The consequences of this are still with us. The lessons which the church has had to learn in the midst of the holocausts of our century compel us to find a new, more profound, more sober, and at the same time more Christian attitude.

Because of the deep and tragic involvement of men of Christian tradition in the persecution of the Jewish people, the cruel and dangerous anti-Jewish attacks in some of the writings of the old Luther, and the continuing threats in our time to the existence of the Jews as a community, we assert our Christian responsibility for their right to exist as Jews.

3. Jews, on their side, insist that there can be mutual respect and dialogue only if the "legitimacy" of Judaism is recognized by Christians. We believe that this includes not only ethnic and political but also religious factors. What does it mean for us to acknowledge its "legitimacy?" Remembering past Christian criticism of Judaism, Jews demand of Christians recognition of Judaism as a "living" religion. Can such recognition be given? Does it mean that we see two separate but necessary ministries within the one economy of salvation? Is it possible to acknowledge that the survival of Judaism is an act of God without also saying that this survival is a definitive event of salvation history? Does affirmation of the survival or acknowledgment of the legitimacy of Judaism cancel the responsibility of the Christian to bear witness to the Jew at the right time and in the proper way?

In the light of these questions we offer the following affirmations:
We as Lutherans affirm our solidarity with the Jewish people. This solidarity is legitimized in God's election and calling into being in Abraham's seed a people of promise, of faith, and of obedience peculiar unto him, a people whose unity will one day become manifest when "all Israel" will be saved. The Lutheran churches, therefore, may not so appropriate the term "people of God" and "Israel" to the church in such a way as to deny that they applied in the first instance to the Jewish people. They may not assert that continuity of the church with the covenant people of Abraham in such a way as to question the fact that present-day Judaism has its own continuity with Old Testament Israel.

Thus our solidarity with the Jewish people is to be affirmed not only despite the crucifixion of Jesus, but also because of it. Through his death Jesus has brought about reconciliation with God, has broken down the barriers between men, and has established a ministry of reconciliation which encompasses all men, both Jews and gentiles.

Thus our solidarity with the Jewish people is grounded in God's unmerited grace, his forgiveness of sin and his justification of the disobedient. Whenever we Christians, therefore, speak about "rejection" and "faith," "disobedience" and "obedience," in such a way that "rejection" and "disobedience" are made to be attributes of Jews while "faith" and "obedience" are made to be attributes of Christians, we are not only guilty of the most despicable spiritual pride, but we foster a pernicious slander, denying the very ground of our own existence: grace, forgiveness, and justification.

After all that has happened, the existence of the Jewish people in the world today cannot therefore be seen in the first instance as a problem to be encountered, much less as an embarrassment to be faced by the churches, but as a profound cause for wonder and hope. Despite all the inhuman actions of men and the frightful ambiguities of history, God remains faithful to his promise. We have here tangible evidence that God's grace is yet at work countering the demonic powers of destruction and guaranteeing a future for mankind which will bring the full unity of God's people.

In understanding ourselves as people of the new covenant which God has made in Jesus the Christ, we Christians see the Jewish people as a reminder of our origin, as a partner in dialogue to understand our common history, and as a living admonition that we too are a pilgrim people, a people enroute toward a goal that can only be grasped in hope. The church, therefore, may never so understand the Word which has been entrusted to it, the Baptism which it must administer, and the Holy Supper which it has been commanded to celebrate as possessions which give Christians superiority over the Jews. The church can only administer in humility the mysteries which God has committed to it—preaching the crucified and risen Christ, baptizing into his death, showing forth his death till he come.

The word which our churches, in bearing witness to Jesus the Christ, must share with Jews as with other men is a joyful message of imperishable hope. This message shows forth a time when God's purpose with his covenant in Abraham and with his covenant in Jesus the Christ will be fulfilled. Then God overcomes all blindness, faithlessness, and disobedience and will be all in all.

2

The Church and
the Jewish People

"The Neuendettelsau Report"

INTRODUCTION BY HAROLD H. DITMANSON

Under the leadership of Dr. Arne Sovik and Dr. Martin Kretzmann, the Neuendettelsau Consultation of the Lutheran World Federation was held in April, 1973. Its purpose was to assess developments that had taken place during the decade since Løgumkloster. Representatives from Lutheran churches in 10 countries met for several days to take an inventory of present Jewish–Christian relationships and to plan for the improvement of such relationships.

This conference had a practical or methodological aim, yet some interesting theological matters were handled. Section I describes the theological burden laid upon the conference by Pastor Reinhard Dobbert. He did not propose answers to questions, nor did he reiterate any classical views of Christian mission. Instead he urged that some fresh thinking be done about the way in which "election" and "justification" are used by synagogue and church to talk about the relationship to God. Pastor Dobbert's essay could be seen as an oblique attack upon the stereotypes of Judaism and Christianity with which Christians have been content for so long. The questions he raised suggest, as Martin Kretzmann wrote in a press release, that Lutherans may be working with presuppositions which have their roots in historical and cultural developments rather than in biblical principles.

There are some significant accents in section II. An increase in the number of interfaith contacts was reported. There were many practical and organizational suggestions for furthering dialogue and improving relationships. The list of possible themes for mutual study contains some interesting items: Judaism as a living religion, our common heritage, dialogue and mission, Luther and the Jews, anti-Semitism in the New Testament, the state of Israel, human rights, peace and justice. Dr. Kretzmann reported that all the participants understood that conversation with our Jewish neighbors must touch upon the state of Israel.

All of these items represent a broadening of Lutheran concerns since the Løgumkloster conference 10 years earlier. In the section entitled "Concerns on the Local Level," (II,F) the question about mission and dialogue is tackled directly. The statement was intended to have a reconciling effect by placing the whole question within a new context. It was hoped that the notion of "caring" would transcend the standard contrasts between mission and nonmission, and between mission and dialogue.

Three levels of caring are indicated: (1) on the level of our common humanity, caring or relationship means to make common cause with Jews in civic and social matters; (2) on the level of concern for minority groups, caring means to give assistance in the struggle against prejudice and discrimination; (3) on the level of religious commitment, caring means a desire to share one's faith. The text at this point (II,F,1,c) speaks to two audiences although no directions are given to the reader. As the author of section II,F, I am quite clear about what those sentences meant to convey. The first four sentences are addressed to any Jewish readers who might examine this document.

Christians should invite Jews to engage in a mutual sharing of faith. Christians are not in a position to tell their Jewish neighbors that they should engage in such activities nor can they prescribe the manner in which this should be done. But Christian faith is marked by the impulse to bear witness to the grace of God in Jesus Christ. To bear such witness is intended as a positive, not a negative act.

The remainder of the paragraph is addressed to a Lutheran audience.

Witness, whether it be called "mission" or "dialogue" includes a desire both to know and to be known more fully. When we speak of a mutual sharing of faith we do not endorse syncretism. . . . We are using the words "witness," "mission," and "dialogue," which have come to be labels for distinctive ways of sharing faith. These words have a different content for different Christians. We see problems in the use of these words and urge that Christian people give attention to exploring their meanings.

I have suggested at an earlier point that an examination of Lutheran statements on Jewish–Christian relations could take the form of an effort to track through these documents the presence of three distinguishable ingredients—a moral imperative, a traditionalist theological perspective (the theology of replacement), and a revisionist theological perspective (the theology of recognition). It is my impression that the Neuendettelsau report contains two of these elements—the moral imperative and a revisionist theology expressed in a low key for the sake of the ongoing harmony of the group enterprise.

THE CHURCH AND THE JEWISH PEOPLE

The Commission on Studies laid down the following lines of work: 1) The furtherance of study work in the member churches and between member churches, collaboration to be sought with other churches and specialized institutes; 2) Cooperation with the World Council of Churches; 3) Consultations or conferences for evaluation of the study work and the exploration of basic theological and methodological questions.

A desk in the Department of Studies was made responsible "to see to it that information channels are open between those working on Jewish–Christian questions in the various member churches, so that there can be direct contact and cooperation if desired."

The report of the Løgumkloster Consultation and other documents produced by the Standing Committee were sent to the member churches for their comments and evaluation with a view to discover those areas which needed further study.

The Commission on Studies saw the possibility that a consultation of concerned persons and representatives of study groups might be necessary in the near future. It expressed the hope "that the consultation will stimulate further work on the question of dialogue between Jews and Christians and Christian–Jewish relations and identify specific issues for continuing study in the churches." Such a consultation was authorized by the commission for 1973. Its aim was to be the furtherance of engagement on the local level, "where good Christian–Jewish relations become manifest, where existential dialogue takes place, where witness is made and where solidarity is shown."

Within the framework of the above guidelines, staff of the Department of Studies made contact with various study groups and laid plans for a consultation whose main aim was to deal with methodology, to bring

35

together persons engaged in various study programs and dialogues with the aim of exchanging information, defining areas of study and suggesting ways in which the Lutheran World Federation might best serve the churches in their ongoing concern for Christian–Jewish relations. In order to keep the consultation small, quotas were set up for each country and the National Committees were asked to appoint representatives to the consultation. Since this was intended primarily as a methodological consultation it was felt that it would not be appropriate to invite representatives of the Jewish community to meet with us at this time.

The consultation carried on its work along two lines:

I. A study section, which included a theological paper and reports from Lutheran study groups, as well as a report on the work being done by the WCC office on the Church and the Jewish People.

II. A practical section in which the consultation divided into three groups to deal with specific recommendations to the Lutheran World Federation, member churches and their congregations, and study groups in the various countries.

I

The basic theological paper under the theme "Election and Justification in View of the Relation Between Church and Synagogue" was presented by Pastor Reinhard Dobbert. He pointed out that this theme stands at the heart of all Christian–Jewish relations and must serve as the framework within which all dialogue takes place. When the church has not taken this question seriously and has dealt with peripheral matters to the exclusion of a clear biblical witness to the meaning of election and justification for both parties in the dialogue, the result has been a distortion of biblical truth and, therefore, a poisoning of relationships. Closely connected with this is the "burning problem of sin-forgiveness."

If Lutheranism is to make a "decisive contribution" to "the further development of the Christian–Jewish dialogue," Pastor Dobbert said, "there must be within Lutheranism certain further studies, which must be concerned with the following questions:

a) What role does the teaching of justification play in the publications of the LWF and the WCC (not only in the area of the Church and the Jewish People)?

b) What distortions of this message are to be found, or where are successful attempts made to express this message in contemporary terms?

c) What sketches, emphases and distortions are there today in general within theology?

d) What is being said today in the church and synagogue on the subject of sin?

e) How is the matter of discontinuity being discussed today in the Synagogue? What role, for example, does the problem of atheism in Israel have?

f) Is the theme of justification (not the concept, but the real thing) even really known in Judaism? Is there, for example, theological thinking done concerning the justification for the political struggle of existence?''

The Rev. Johan Snoek of the WCC had been requested by staff to prepare a response to the Dobbert paper. Pastor Snoek pointed out that it is unrealistic to say that "Christendom must repeatedly attempt to speak with one voice." There is a plurality of voices among Jews as well as Christians. "Even within the different denominations there are deep divisions. We should not sweep differences under the carpet by trying to speak 'with one voice' but rather bring tensions out in the open and try to deal sensibly with them.''

It was pointed out that the essayist himself had said that the Lutheran Church did not regard the "doctrine of election and justification of mankind in Christ Jesus" as the "proprium" of Lutheranism but as a "proprium of the Christian message." Rather than speak of a specific "Lutheran contribution" to the Jewish–Christian dialogue, would it not be better to speak of a "special benefit" for Lutherans to be derived from the dialogue with the Jews? Lutherans might benefit greatly in such concepts as "two dominions," "law and Gospel," and "justification" through dialogue with Jews.

Pastor Snoek pointed out that if the essayist is correct in stating that the Church must be in "a constant discussion with the Synagogue, for without this vis-à-vis the church is in constant danger of misunderstanding its own nature," then "the special concerns of this consultation and of this paper should be exposed to the criticism of those who—though committed Christians—do not share this concern for Christian–Jewish dialogue."

The full text of Pastor Dobbert's paper and Pastor Snoek's response are available from Geneva on request.

Since May 1971 the WCC office has involved the churches in a study program on the subject of "Biblical Interpretation and its Bearing on Christian Attitudes Regarding the Situation in the Middle East." It was felt that such a study might serve "to avoid misuse of the Bible in support of partisan views." Christians are deeply divided in their evaluation of the situation in the Middle East. An analysis of their biblical assumptions may enable "the Church to be more effectively an instrument of reconciliation" since their "present divergencies paralyze the churches' efforts in this respect." It is one of the aims of the program to bring together people of divergent viewpoints so that differences can be faced honestly and openly and, even though such differences may not be resolved, possibilities for common action might be found.

Pastor Snoek pointed out that there is deep polarization in the church between those who support a "theology of the land" and see in recent historic events a fulfillment of Old Testament promises, and those who espouse a "theology of the poor" and, therefore, side with the Palestinian refugees. Another important factor in the discussion is the difference of conceptions regarding the relationship of the Old and the New Testament.

In order to help the study groups, a 17-point questionnaire was drawn up. Study groups have been established in Finland, Sweden, Norway, Denmark, Germany and France. Material was also received from Israel and Lebanon. Many Lutheran groups participated in this study. A notable gap in the program was the absence of any study groups on this subject in North America.

Pastor Snoek also reported on the program of dialogue with Jewish leaders which is carried on by the World Council of Churches. In 1965 and 1968 informal meetings were held between representatives of the WCC and a number of Jewish leaders. An "International Jewish Committee on Interreligious Consultations" was set up. Since 1970 regular meetings of the two groups have been held. Apart from the discussion of religious themes, an important aspect of these meetings has been the discussion of general themes in which Christians and Jews have common interests as fellow members of the human community. Such themes as the problems of violence, racism in Southern Africa, human rights in the Soviet Union, the Middle East conflict, and the Bible and social justice, have established a climate of mutual and common concern which fosters good will and cooperation.

The participants in the consultation expressed their interest in the work of the WCC and their deep appreciation of what is being done through that office on behalf of the Lutheran churches as well. It was pointed out that some of the churches make only a minimal contribution to that work and some do not contribute at all. The consultation felt that the WCC office was carrying out this program also on behalf of the Lutheran churches and did much to further their concerns for the Jewish people. For this reason the consultation resolved to recommend to the various national committees that they allocate grants to the work which Pastor Snoek is doing in the

World Council while at the same time continuing their support of the parallel and supplementary work done in the Lutheran World Federation.

II

The following recommendations given here are the text which was adopted by the consultation as a whole.

A. On the Work of the Church and the Jewish People in General

The members of this consultation are convinced that the relation of the church with the Jewish people is so important for the Christian self-understanding and for the whole church, and the improvement of relationships so crucial, that studies and work in this area must be intensified. In this connection we recall that the Commission on Studies of the Lutheran World Federation has set the following guidelines for the furtherance of studies on the church and the Jewish people. The Commission on Studies sees its work in this field being done along three lines:

1. The furtherance of study work in the member churches and between member churches, collaboration to be sought with other churches and specialized institutes;

2. Cooperation with the World Council of Churches;

3. Consultations or conferences for evaluation of the study work and the exploitation of basic theological and methodological questions.

B. On Structuring of Studies

1. We have discussed in detail the organizational form for studies in this area of concern: in the LWF Commission and Department of Studies; on the national level; through task forces; and on the local level.

It is *recommended* that further group work take place, if possible in the form of a new committee, in any event in task forces with specific assignments.

In this connection a new consultation along the lines described in Guidelines point 3 above should be planned for the near future.

2. We are grateful for the work which the Commission on Studies of the LWF has previously accomplished in this area. We are convinced, however, that the expanding work outlined under (1) above can be successfully carried forward only if suitable staff assistance is provided. The members of this consultation therefore *request* the LWF for provision for staff assistance for this area of concern. At the same time the request is

made of the national committees (or similar organizations) to support this request as emphatically as possible (especially financial support). Several organizations represented at this consultation have already indicated a willingness to help financially in this particular project.

The functions for this staff assignment would include: furtherance and coordination of studies on various levels; preparation for study groups and consultations; evaluation and publication of study materials; cooperation with the corresponding office in the World Council of Churches, as well as with national and local groups and institutes; a central clearing house for literature and information.

C. On Methodology for Studies and Conversation

Distinction must be made among intra-Lutheran discussion, interconfessional dialogue, and conversations with Jews. For the themes (mentioned below) for study, the following points ought to be noted: In the present situation, what is important for Christian–Jewish conversation? (What is already included in the conversation? What should be included in the future?) What questions must Lutherans clarify further among themselves with reference to conversation with Jews?

D. On Themes for Study and Conversation

Among the major areas and themes the following are significant:

1. Church and Synagogue
God-talk (how we speak to God);
Election, Covenant, and People of God;
Judaism as a living religion;
The relation of the Old Testament and the New;
Sin, guilt, and suffering;
Jewish and Christian anthropology;
Our common heritage.

For us, further clarification of our understanding of justification, law, and especially Christology is necessary with regard to these above questions.

2. Dialogue and Mission
Various ways and levels of encounter and conversation;
Goal and aim (including the question of conversion, proselytism,

and witness);
Media (literature, etc.).

3. *The State of Israel*
   "Promise" (with reference to the land);
   Jewish and Arab minorities in the Middle East.

4. *Anti-Semitism*
   Luther and the Jews;
   Anti-Semitism in the New Testament;
   Anti-Semitism in modern literature, textbooks, worship, materials, etc.

5. *General Themes*
   The search for World Community;
   Human rights;
   Peace and justice;
   Cooperation with communities of persons of other faiths;
   Problems of violence;
   Problems of racism.

The discussion of these general themes is suggested because it is hoped that Christian–Jewish conversation will not only deal with issues of direct interest to the Jewish and Christian communities but will also seek to serve the wider community of mankind.

E. On "Jerusalem"

In the view of the concern of the Neuendettelsau Consultation on the Church and the Jewish People for the presence of the Lutheran Church in the Holy Land we submit the following.
Recommendations:
1. Information has reached this conference that at a recent synod meeting of the Evangelical Lutheran Church in Jordan it was decided to apply for membership in the LWF. This Consultation rejoices in this decision and encourages the LWF Executive Committee to give serious consideration to this application for membership, recognizing how important it is that the Evangelical Lutheran Church in Jordan established active relationship with the worldwide Lutheran family.
2. The Commission on Studies be asked to request the LWF Executive Committee to authorize an early consultation of representatives of the LWF

Commissions as well as local representatives from the Holy Land area and their supporting constituents for open discussion on such issues as follows:

a) The proposed Lutheran Centre in Jerusalem. (This Consultation felt that such a centre should not be a competing educational institute but should encourage cooperation with educational program facilities available in the area such as the Swedish Theological Institute, the Ecumenical Institute, the Hebrew University, etc.)

b) The future use of the Augusta Victoria Foundation Hospital.

c) The necessity of a Lutheran Representative in the area. The proposed consultation should assume responsibility to prepare a job description for this position.

There will be other issues that should be added to the agenda which we are not prepared to identify now (e.g. certain items in the report of the former LWF Committee on the Church and the Jewish People to the Fifth Assembly of LWF).

This Consultation recommends that, in preparation for the proposed "Jerusalem" consultation, talks should be initiated between representatives of the different Lutheran groups in Israel and representatives of the LWF.

3. We note that some Christians in the Holy Land face anxieties and difficulties because of their faith. Where assistance and encouragement from the LWF might help people to remain to work out their Christian calling, we suggest that this be provided. This will require some special research and study on the part of the LWF.

4. The Commission on Studies be asked to encourage the General Secretariat of the LWF to seek to obtain "personal status" as a church for the Lutheran congregations in Israel.

5. We have been advised by Rev. Terray that the Norwegian Israel Mission, in cooperation with other Lutheran agencies, plans to build an old peoples' home on LWF property in Haifa, presently housing worship facilities for the Lutheran Congregation there. We commend these cooperating Lutheran agencies for reaching out to meet this need. *We recommend* that the Board of Trustees of the LWF endorse this extended use of LWF property in Haifa.

F. On Concerns on the Local Level

Certain aspects of Christian–Jewish relations are of primary importance for local congregations and national churches. These issues and activities must be pursued on the local level, with some assistance and direction given by national church offices and agencies. The problems and activities to which we call attention will vary in nature from one country to another, but we believe there are common elements which represent the interest of all participants in this Consultation.

1. We urge that Christian congregations should care for their Jewish neighbors and should seek to establish relationships with them. We see three levels of caring or relationship:

a) On the level of our common humanity, Christian people should take the initiative in promoting friendly relationships with their Jewish neighbors. As fellow-citizens, Jews and Christians have common problems and obligations. Wherever possible and desirable Christians should make common cause with Jews in matters of civic and social concern. Mutual acquaintance and respect are essential to the well-being of both Christians and Jews.

b) On the level of concern for minority groups, Christians should give all possible assistance to their Jewish neighbors in the struggle against prejudice, discrimination, and persecution. Without sharing a common creed, Jews and Christians may cooperate to the fullest extent in fostering human rights.

c) On the level of religious commitment, Christians should invite Jews to engage in a mutual sharing of faith. Christians are not in a position to tell their Jewish neighbors that they should engage in such activities nor can they prescribe the manner in which this should be done. But Christian faith is marked by the impulse to bear witness to the grace of God in Jesus Christ. To bear such witness is intended as a positive, not a negative act. Witness, whether it be called "mission" or "dialogue," includes a desire both to know and to be known more fully. When we speak of a mutual sharing of faith we do not endorse syncretism. But we understand that when Christians and Jews speak to each other about matters of faith, there will be an exchange which calls for openness, honesty, love, and mutual respect. One cannot reveal his faith to another without recognizing the real differences that exist and being willing to take the risk of confronting these differences. We are using the words "witness," "mission," and "dialogue," which have come to be labels for distinctive ways of sharing faith. These words have a different content for different Christians. We see problems in the use of these words and urge that Christian people give attention to exploring their meanings.

Although these relationships must be established on the local level, with assistance from national offices and agencies, *we recommend* that the LWF promote these activities by facilitating the exchange of information and materials on the international level.

2. In the light of the increasing number of interfaith marriages in several countries, we believe that new dimensions and approaches in pastoral counseling are urgent. Such interfaith marriages may lead to the

conversion of one partner or the other, or they may lead to the breaking of connections with both synagogue and church, or they may become cells for ongoing Christian–Jewish dialogue. We do not urge that interfaith marriages be seen as another means of promoting conversions to the Christian faith. But we do wish to urge that the churches should be aware of the increasing need for a special kind of pastoral help for the sake of strengthening the unity of families and the faith of individuals. This need should be met by new techniques in the training of pastors.

We urge that the LWF transmit this concern to the appropriate agencies.

3. We urge that the churches have an important educational task to perform in the area of Jewish–Christian relations.

a) We reaffirm the message of the Løgumkloster Declaration with respect to the importance of continuing the struggle against anti-Semitism in any form. We note with approval that during recent years several member churches of the LWF have made substantial progress in the effort to remove from Christian publications false and misleading statements about Jews. These efforts have often been made in consultation with Jewish scholars. We must continue to oppose the "teaching of contempt" wherever it may be found.

We urge that churches should produce and offer suitable materials for religious education both in church schools and, wherever possible, in public schools. It is also necessary that churches should design programs of instruction aimed at changing the attitudes of teachers who use these materials.

We recommend that the LWF transmit this concern to member churches.

b) We recognize the phenomenon of tourism today, especially the increase of travel to the Holy Land. Many of these tours are advertised as "Lutheran" enterprises. We believe that such travel and exposure can have both positive and negative results with respect to intergroup relationships and interfaith understanding. For the benefit of such tourists and their leaders we encourage Lutheran publishing houses to give special attention to the preparation of informative materials which will provide an accurate, balanced, and reconciling picture of the situation in the Middle East today. We recognize that some churches have already produced useful publications. We recommend that agencies of the national churches take further initiatives in the preparation of such materials and find ways of making them available to tourists and travel agencies. Such action would do much to prevent misunderstanding and to increase the positive results of travel. *We recommend* that the LWF serve as the channel for the international exchange of such materials.

3

The Oneness of God and the Uniqueness of Christ: Christian Witness and the Jewish People

"The Oslo Report"

INTRODUCTION BY HAROLD H. DITMANSON

When we turn to the third Lutheran World Federation statement, the Oslo report of 1975, we return to the theological ideas that were introduced at Løgumkloster. In the introduction to the report, Dr. Arne Sovik explained the nature and aim of the consultation. The Oslo conference was designed to provide a forum in which Lutherans could face their disagreements about Jewish–Christian relations and especially about the Christian witness to Jewish people. Sovik pointed out that this diversity of opinion is rooted in historical and cultural circumstances but that in the long run the interpretation of Scripture is the most important source of disagreement.

The specific problem to be considered by the consultation is described in the preface. Do certain theological, biblical, and historical factors "require that Christians' conversation with Jews and witness to them be in some way 'special' "? This way of approaching the question of mission already shows an openness to revisionist themes that is not found in sections I and II of the Løgumkloster report. As Arne Sovik and Paul Opsahl put the question, the implication is present that Lutherans can legitimately answer yes or no to the "theology of replacement." Sovik and Opsahl summarized the intended message of the report by underlining its positive attitude towards Jewish people and by pointing to the missionary impulse which is an intrinsic part of Christian faith. It is significant that in this brief summary no mention is made of a conversionary aim or hope in relation to Jews.

In our examination of Lutheran documents we have focused on the tension between the historic theology of replacement and the more recent theology of recognition. It is my impression that in the Løgumkloster report both perspectives are strongly stated. In the Neuendettelsau report the theology of recognition prevails, and in the Oslo report the theology of replacement is dominant. The classic theology of replacement is evident in section I. Parts A and B set forth the historic Christian view of the relation between the Jewish and the Christian Scriptures. Christians share the Jewish faith in the one God who is Creator and Redeemer. But Christians must associate this faith in God with acceptance of Jesus Christ as the crucified and risen Messiah, to whom the Old Testament bears witness, and who is the only way of salvation for all humankind, both Jews and Gentiles.

Although Judaism does not understand its own Bible correctly and therefore diverges from Christianity at the point of Christology, it is still the case that a relationship continues to exist between the two faiths in their common use of the Hebrew Scriptures. More than that, Paul said in Romans 9–11 that God has not disowned his people, that Christians should not feel superior to Jews, and that one day all who belong to God will be gathered together.

This "relationship" is said to involve a "mutual challenge." Christians challenge Jews to accept Christ as the only true way to God. This is not said explicitly in part C, but the logic of the text requires this idea, and it has been said at an earlier point. On the other hand, Jews are explicitly said to challenge Christians at three points. First, they bear witness to monotheism and thus warn Christians against slipping into either polytheism or Jesus-ism. Second, Judaism helps Christianity to take the humanness of Jesus seriously. Third, Judaism in its devotion to God's law reminds Christians of the importance of moral obligation.

It is significant that in the "reciprocal challenge" Christianity announces to Judaism the one way to a saving relationship with God, while Judaism reminds Christianity to take more seriously elements that are intrinsically Christian—the oneness of God, the humanity of Jesus, moral obedience. Many readers would come to the conclusion that such a "challenge" is hardly "reciprocal" or "mutual." It is surely an asymmetrical relationship when Christians offer Jews the truth and Jews offer Christians some useful reminders. Such a scheme cannot be seen as interaction between two living religions. Christianity does the giving and Judaism does the receiving *because* it is incomplete and has been replaced as a form of saving contact with God. It is for these reasons that I said earlier that in the Oslo report the theology of replacement overwhelms the theology of recognition. This impression is heightened when we turn to section II. It is difficult to analyze the section on "Christian Witness" in terms of interlocking steps in a chain of reasoning. Since the sections were originally drafted by different task forces, they differ from each other in theological presuppositions and style of expression. There are parts of section II which were no doubt clear to their authors and to some others but are not clear to me. As I work my way through the text, however, I do find a definite disavowal of the notion that Christians and Jews are related as "haves" and "have-nots." There is sensitivity in this disavowal, although it is hardly consistent with the argument of section I. The rationale for this posture of humility is that all mission is God's mission and Christians stand with all others under the divine word of judgment and salvation. It follows from this that Jews are neither to be singled out nor left out by the Christian mission. Nothing is said about the exact form such a policy would take.

But whatever form mission might take, the impulse to witness grows out of the fact that Christians are the only ones who know that God saves the world through Christ. Christians have knowledge to share with those who do not have it, even though the knowledge is about God's grace and the solidarity of Christians with all humankind. Nothing is said about whether Jews or adherents of other religions have anything to share with Christians. The implication is that Christians have something to tell but nothing to learn. So section II does agree with section I in denying that there can be the sort of mutual sharing of faith recommended by the Neuendettelsau report.

Sensitivity continues to be mixed with a theology of replacement as part B affirms that the form of Christian witness to Jews must take account of special circumstances. That is, we must wrestle with the paradox of continuity and discontinuity that marks the encounter between Judaism and Christianity. The commitment to mission cannot be evaded even though it must not be carried out in a patronizing manner or in a spirit of superiority. It appears therefore that section II also presupposes the theology of re-placement. There is little of the openness one finds in Løgumkloster and Vatican II.

In section III one senses a quite different atmosphere. The suspicion that one is in the presence of a different drafting committee is well founded. This section was originally written by Professor Krister Stendahl and ex-pressed a point of view he was especially interested in conveying to and through the consultation. In its original form it had the qualities of candor and vividness one always finds in Stendahl's writing. The content belongs chiefly to what I have called the moral level. Yet there were enough traces of a nontraditional theological position shining through his remarks about mistakes Lutherans had made and should not make again to cause uneasiness among the supporters of sections I and II.

Dr. Stendahl's draft ran into heavy weather. He was not disposed to back down on matters of deep theological conviction and declined to have a hand in any further revisions. With his consent, however, the draft was turned over to an editor who changed the text in such a way that the special concerns of Dean Stendahl and Dr. George Forell could be preserved even while they were formulated in language that the critics of the draft could accept. With a few revisions in the plenary session, the compromise statement was accepted even though it was still too strong for some and too weak for others. To put it very briefly, section III is a confession of guilt, a plea for humility, a declaration of solidarity, a pledge to take responsible action with respect to the anti-Semitism that leads to holocausts, and a call to find ways of effecting reconciliation in the Middle East.

Section IV is practical in nature. It calls upon Lutherans to put into practice, through coherent organizational procedures, the commitments they had made to their Jewish neighbors over the past 10 years. I drafted this section on the basis of dozens of specific suggestions made by individuals and subcommittees. I will not attempt to summarize this section since it is already a rather skeletal presentation of many practical steps to be taken. In the interest, however, of our overall focus on the mix of ethical and theological components in Lutheran statements, it is worth noting that all four sections of the Oslo report stress the element of moral obligation, while sections I and II presuppose the traditional theology of replacement, and sections III and IV, a theology of recognition.

The tension between differing theological perspectives that appeared in the Løgumkloster statement is still present in the Oslo report. It is clear that Lutherans have wrestled with the theme of continuity and discontinuity, as urged in section II of the Oslo statement. The lengthy debates have not produced a consensus among Lutherans, nor is it likely that they will do so in the future. Religious convictions do not lend themselves to consensus statements. Since the God whom we worship and upon whose activity we reflect is an infinite being who exceeds the measure of the human mind, it happens that the subject matter of theology overflows definite categories and escapes being ultimately comprehended. So it is not surprising that there should be rather pronounced differences of interpretation within the Christian community. One group sees more clearly than another the meaning of one or another side of the Christian faith. But no one sees the whole

Christian faith at once and in perfect balance. Thus it is that the most important outcome of the recent dialogue within Lutheranism is the legitimation of theological pluralism with respect to Jewish–Christian relations. Lutheran churches have officially endorsed the coexistence of diverse perspectives and programs. Faithful men and women can follow in freedom the light they believe God has given them.

THE ONENESS OF GOD AND THE UNIQUENESS OF CHRIST: CHRISTIAN WITNESS AND THE JEWISH PEOPLE

Introduction by Arne Sovik

The papers that follow were prepared for a consultation held in Oslo, Norway, in late August 1975, under the sponsorship of the Department of Studies of the Lutheran World Federation.

The Oslo Consultation was the third general consultation on the subject of the church and the Jewish people held under LWF sponsorship. At Løgumkloster, Denmark, in 1964 some forty theologians and mission leaders made a first attempt at an international Lutheran conference to discover what might be the special responsibilities that Lutherans might have toward the Jewish people, what solutions might be suggested for the exegetical and theological problems that burden our understanding of Christian–Jewish relations, and what our churches might do to divest themselves of the elements of anti-Semitism that have, to our shame, been present among Lutherans ever since the Reformation. A small group continued to work until 1969 on the theological issues and produced a short paper for the Assembly of 1970.

A second meeting was called in Neuendettelsau, German Federal Republic, in 1973, more to assess the developments in the last decade and ask questions for the future than to deal with specific issues. It was clear to all who were there, as it must be clear to anyone who has read material on the subject, that Lutherans are by no means of one mind when it comes to an understanding of Christian–Jewish relations, not least as concerns the Christian witness. The reasons for this diversity are historical and cultural as well as theological. The grounds for the last of these lie ultimately in the difficulty of interpreting Scripture. They focus both on the cryptic passages in Romans 9–11 and on the meaning of the New Testament claims for the finality of Jesus. It seemed good therefore to a group which was considering what steps ought next to be taken within Lutheranism to move toward greater common understanding that the first problem for us should not be an attempt to deal with the urgent and practical issues of the Middle East and the place of Israel in the modern world. Rather there should be an attempt to deal exegetically and theologically with the scriptural testimony, acknowledging the fact that Scripture is interpreted, under the influence of historical exigencies. The ultimate choice of theme and the procedures of the historical exigencies. The ultimate choice of theme and the procedures of the Oslo Consultation need not be dealt with here since they are treated briefly in the Report.

We here express our gratitude to the scholars who prepared the papers, and then revised them for publication here. Some were prepared in German, and we accept responsibility for any inadequacies of translation. It is to our regret that an illuminating and scholarly paper on the history of Jewish life in the Nordic countries, which was presented by Dr. Oskar Mendelssohn, a leader of the Oslo Jewish community, could not be included.

Thanks are also due to Mr. M. L. Kretzmann, whose health made it impossible for him to participate in a consultation for which he had done the initial preparatory work, and to Dr. Paul Opsahl, whose levelheaded chairmanship gave both freedom and purposiveness to the discussions.

Preface

From August 25–30, 1975, at the Voksenasen Conference Center in Oslo, Norway, thirty persons gathered to discuss "The Oneness of God and the Uniqueness of Christ: Christian Witness and the Jewish People." This was the third international consultation on the church and the Jewish people convened under the auspices of the Lutheran World Federation. The following statement will be most fully understood when studied in light of the earlier deliberations: Løgumkloster, Denmark (1964) together with a subsequent committee report (1969) and Neuendettelsau, Germany (1973).

From a broad selection of issues requiring further study (which had been developed in Neuendettelsau) a preparatory committee had chosen one in which there was known to be considerable disagreement among Lutherans, namely, the nature of the Christian conversation with the Jewish people. Do our common faith in One God, our common heritage in the Old Testament, the Christian recognition that a special place is accorded Israel in the New Testament as in the Old, and the long and problematic history of Christian–Jewish relations require that Christians' conversation with Jews and witness to them be in some way "special"? If so, in what way, theologically and practically? The theme of the Oslo Consultation and its subject matter were developed with this problem in mind. It was seen as primarily a matter of biblical interpretation and application. Its treatment could obviously have important implications for all our thinking about Christian mission.

In preparation for discussion a number of papers were presented, some in thetic form. Professor Harold Ditmanson, Northfield, Minnesota, USA, dealt with influences which have affected our understanding of the Jewish people throughout the history of the church. Dr. Jukka Thuren, Turku, Finland, discussed the oneness of God as seen in both Old and New Testaments. Dean Magne Saebo, Oslo, Norway, and Dean Krister Stendahl, Cambridge, Massachusetts, USA, approached the topic, "No Other Name" (Acts 4:12), from the standpoints of the Old and New Testaments respectively. Professor Christopher Burchard, Heidelberg, Germany, examined the concepts of proclamation and witness (*kerygma* and *martyria*) in the New Testament. (The texts of most of these papers are available on request, in German or English.)

Group Bible studies on passages relating to the biblical papers preceded each of those presentations. The latter half of the week was devoted chiefly to work in three groups from which the basic content of the following statement emerged. Each portion of this report was discussed, redrafted, and then accepted at the concluding plenary session.

Significant personal and informational exchange occurred during one evening session when several members of the Oslo Jewish community met with consultation participants. Dr. Oskar Mendelssohn, author of a history of the Jews in Norway, presented a paper on the Jewish experience in the Nordic countries. Further conversation led to a frank discussion of such issues as mission and dialogue, and the place and image of Jews and Judaism in Christian teaching.

Consultation participants are aware that there are a number of critical contemporary questions which this report does not address, or address as thoroughly as some might have hoped. In certain instances this was because these questions fell outside the purview of this consultation's thematic focus. On other matters, differing views among participants could not be resolved within the time framework of the meeting.

Early in the consultation, however, one participant drew attention to an old axiom for good homiletics: we are not so much responsible for *what* we say, or what we think we say, but what we are *heard* to say. It is to be hoped that this report conveys to all readers the capacity to regard Jewish people with high honor, love, and a sense of eschatological wonder, as well as bear a clear witness to the name and honor of Jesus Christ, and the centrality of his crucifixion and resurrection.

This report is presented to the Commission of Studies of the LWF. The statement of the consultation does not speak for the Lutheran World Federation. Rather, it speaks to the Federation; it expresses the mind of a group of Lutherans assembled under LWF auspices to deliberate on a theme, and reports back to that body. In consequence of the strong conviction of the consultation that unless the study programs of the Federation "have some practical consequences on regional and local levels, the studies will have been made in vain," this document is also being sent to LWF member churches with the request that it be studied, reflected upon and acted upon as the nature of the situation requires.

Participants in the consultation would not let it go unnoticed if we failed to include in this report expression of their appreciation to those whose efforts made the consultation a possibility and a pleasure: The Norwegian Israel Mission, local host, secretaries, stewards, interpreters, the Voksenasen staff and representatives of the Church of Norway. Costs were met in part by grants from the USA, Canadian and German National Committees of the LWF and from the Norwegian Israel Mission.

PAUL D. OPSAHL,   ARNE SOVIK, Staff
Chairman Division of   Department of Studies
Theological Studies   Lutheran World Federation
Lutheran Council in the U.S.A.

Statement of the Consultation

I. The Oneness of God and the Uniqueness of Christ

A. The Oneness of God

When we as Christians speak about God we refer to the God to whom Holy Scripture bears witness. He revealed himself to His chosen people of Israel, and we are indebted to them for this witness. The conviction that God is one, claiming exclusive allegiance, matured in them from the beginning and they hold to it through many periods of danger and suffering. In this, Israel was always different from the other nations, who acknowledged and worshiped a number of gods.

Together with the Jews, we confess the one God.

The fundamental Jewish confession of faith, the *Shema Yisrael* ("Hear, O Israel, the Lord our God is one Lord" Deut. 6:4), is the obvious background of the Christian creed. We also share the Jews' faith in God's creative power over the whole world and in His will to save all mankind as attested in the Old Testament.

B. The Uniqueness of Christ

Christians make those statements only in conjunction with the affirmation that for them faith in the one God is indissolubly linked with confessing the uniqueness of Jesus Christ. Thus they witness to and call upon the one God as the Father of Jesus Christ.

The conviction of the first Christians that the final realization of the Kingdom of God had begun in Jesus Christ was grounded in and strengthened by encounter with the risen Christ. That the crucified one is the Messiah through whom came salvation and redemption has always remained basic to the Christian faith and was exuberantly expressed in the statement of the early church: "And there is salvation in no one else, for there is no other name under heaven given among men by which we must be saved" (Acts 4:12).

In this conviction, Christians began to discover and read the Scriptures in a new way. A variety of Old Testament affirmations on the way of salvation were brought into focus and related directly to Jesus in the attempt to describe the experience of his uniqueness. They thereby confessed Jesus as the way to the Father for all mankind, both Jews and Gentiles.

C. Judaism and Christianity: A Mutual Challenge

This statement of faith marked the parting of the ways for Jews and Christians. However, a relationship between Judaism and the church still remains. The fact that both move forward from the same Old Testament starting point is a constant reciprocal challenge for Christians and Jews.

Paul was concerned with the special relationship between Christians and Jews in his letter to the Romans. Chapters 9–11 bear witness to his grappling with this question. He emphasizes that God has not disowned his people. He warns the Gentile Christians against arrogance vis-à-vis the Jews, and expects a final gathering of all those who belong to God.

In the postbiblical age the Christian doctrine of the triune God and the true humanity and divinity of Christ was developed on the basis of the rich store of New Testament statements about the uniqueness of Jesus Christ. This doctrine is meant to express and preserve faith in the one God in light of the overwhelming experience of the uniqueness of Jesus Christ and the power of the Holy Spirit. Hence the Nicene Creed opens with the words, "We believe in one God. . . ."

But, this doctrine has not always protected us against misunderstandings. For example, the experience of the uniqueness of Jesus Christ and the concentration of all statements of faith on him have not infrequently resulted in giving all attention to Jesus, thus tending to eclipse God. His will to be the way to the Father is thereby obscured, as is also his will to return his kingdom to the Father at the end (1 Cor. 15:24-28).

The existence of Judaism poses a continuing question as to whether we as Christians keep our faith in the one God. Christian–Jewish conversation can help to avoid imprecise speech about God. This is important for all Christian language about Him.

When Jews concern themselves with Jesus, he is seen as a man. This can help us as Christians to take Jesus' humanity completely seriously. In Judaism particular importance is attached to the obedience which is realized in just actions. Judaism thus reminds Christianity that the one God wants our witness to Him not only in word, but also in deed.

II. Christian Witness

A. The Nature of Christian Witness

Christians need to remember that their witness to the Jewish people is but part and parcel of their witness to all people. There has sometimes been the misperception that Jews are to be isolated in a class by themselves, and then either singled out for exclusive missionary attention or excluded from Christian mission altogether. But this would assume that Jews are qualitatively different from ourselves, and furthermore that it is something about ourselves—perhaps that we are the have's and others are the have-not's—that generates Christian witness. That would be to forget that Christian witness, whether to Judaism or to anyone else, is God's mission and not our own. Christians, no less than others, are sinners and share in the common crisis of all mankind under divine judgment. "We are beggars," said Luther, and all we have is pure gift.

Christians have always been witnessing to their faith. "As the Father sent me, so I send you" (John 22:21). But what that very sending reminds us is that salvation in Christ is an action of God embracing all mankind. It is God who saves the world. The Christians through their witness only share the benefits of this salvation and the good news about it. They know that in Christ Jesus God has already deeded those gifts to all mankind, and not only to those who happen already to be enjoying them.

B. Christian Witness and the Jewish People

The Christian witness is directed toward all our fellowman, including the Jewish people. In witnessing to Jews, however, we must be mindful of the unique historical and spiritual relationship we have with them, both in continuity and discontinuity.

Among Jewish people, no Christian witness would suffice which does not gratefully affirm and live out what they and we have in common. Yet it is that very continuity between us which intensifies the discontinuity. To minimize this unique discontinuity, therefore, would likewise be evasive and artificial. The coming of Christ and the challenge of his gospel place Judaism in a situation of crisis. No Christian witness can be unsympathetic with that, seeing how Christians themselves face a similar crisis before the same Christ. Having done so as Christians, however, they cannot abandon the New Testament proclamation even though they must recognize that that proclamation continues to put contemporary Judaism under the same original challenge. Yet there is only one way for Christian witness to share in that ordeal, namely, in the same compassion and solidarity with the hearers that Christ has displayed toward Christians themselves, and with the same concern he has for every aspect of the hearer's entire well-being.

III. Jewish–Christian Relations: Repentance and Hope

This topic has been studied carefully in the past and has been described in several documents previously issued by the LWF, its member churches, and other Christian bodies. In what follows we intend to offer some suggestions which will serve as addenda to these statements.

When we speak of the guilt and responsibility of Lutherans and other Christians in having fostered and allowed anti-Semitism, we should not give the impression that Christianity is simply identified with the old "Western" (and "Eastern") churches. The arrogant habit of describing Western experience as if it were global must be discontinued. The churches of Asia and Africa have not had the same part in this sordid history. We urge them, however, to define and expose the potential or actual forms of anti-Semitism that may be theirs.

We Lutherans must be aware of our peculiar forms of potential and actual anti-Semitism. An undiscriminating disparagement of the Law in our theology, preaching, instruction, and piety frequently has as its tragic result a caricaturing of the Jew as the epitome of hypocrisy and works-righteousness to the point of putting the label of "Judaizing" upon the common human tendency towards legalism. This fact emphasizes the need to study this problem and to invite Jewish scholars to examine our materials for this kind of anti-Semitism.

Jesus said: "If you are offering your gift at the altar, and there remember that your brother has something against you . . . " (Matthew 5:23). Not least in Jewish–Christian relations is this word an important one. For here the question is not only about *our* feelings of love and *our* rights to witness, but also of whether others have something against us. That is why we must listen to the Jewish community. We must sense their pain and hear their voice on the question of the threat and reality of anti-Semitism and of how to improve Jewish–Christian relations. Christian documents are by now rich in admissions of guilt for past sins. Some of our Jewish friends will tell us that our guilt feelings do them little good. They may benefit us even less. Our repentance is worthy of the name only if it leads to change, to renewed hope, to prayer and work for a better future. An essential stop is to ask our Jewish neighbors what hurts them. A rabbinic story tells of the excited student who said to his teacher, "Rabbi, I love you." The rabbi replied, "Do you know what hurts me?" The student answered, "No." The rabbi asked, "How then can you say that you love me?"

The conflict in the Middle East raises difficult questions about the future of the Jewish people, the rights of Palestinian Arabs and the problems of all refugees. Lutherans and other Christians are painfully aware of the fact that Christianity has for 19 centuries been a source of anti-Semitic thought and action. We cannot confess our guilty involvement in the Holocaust of the 1940s without committing ourselves to action that will prevent the repetition of such a tragedy. We must say, "Never again!" We know that the right to live cannot be securely enjoyed unless peace is achieved. We therefore call upon Lutheran churches to make responsible contributions toward the achievement of peace and reconciliation, justice and dignity, among all the peoples of the Middle East.

IV. Prospects for the Future

It has been the practice of Lutherans to approach their responsibilities by giving careful attention to the biblical and theological aspects of problems. The topic of Lutheran-Jewish relationships for example has been studied over a long period of time by individual scholars, and during the past decade several significant statements have been issued by Lutheran churches in various countries and by Lutheran World Federation conferences. Those statements do not constitute a final or complete treatment of the topic, but they have spoken to the important questions and indicate a growing concern among Lutherans.

At this point, it is easy to say that further study should be given to many topics. Some of these topics need to be clarified among Lutherans and others should be discussed with representatives of the Jewish community. We have in mind such themes as election, covenant, and the people of God; Judaism as a living religion; the relation of the Old Testament and the New; the significance of the law; sin, guilt, and suffering; Jewish and Christian anthropology; the goals, aims, and procedures of mission and dialogue; the historical and present dimensions and remedies of anti-Semitism; the theological and moral implications of the Holocaust; the meaning of Judaism for Christian self-understanding; the significance of the state of Israel in its Middle Eastern context; and the search for peace, justice, and human rights throughout the human community. Such topics will always need further study and will no doubt continue to be examined by individuals and groups. Emphasis should now be placed upon the *dissemination* and *use* of studies and declarations that are our common possession. In the pursuit of this objective, European and American committees are now able to give more effective leadership in the collection, interpretation, and distribution of useful study documents.

Unless Lutheran position papers have some practical consequences on regional and local levels, the studies will have been made in vain. We believe that the process of study, publication, and interaction with other Lutherans and Jews should continue regionally and locally. But we also believe that the Lutheran World Federation can perform essential services for its member churches as all Lutherans work together to deepen their sense of solidarity with the sufferings of the Jewish people. We therefore urge the Lutheran World Federation, through its appropriate offices, to:

1) Maintain contact between groups in several continents which are conducting studies and formulating policies with respect to Lutheran–Jewish relations. Commissions have already been formed in Europe and America which have the function of furthering the exchange of studies and information, and promoting engagement in common projects. This work is being carried out in the form of working parties, study conferences, and publications. These commissions will coordinate these tasks within the churches so far as it is desirable and possible.

2) Cooperate in all possible ways with the World Council of Churches' Committee on the Church and the Jewish People and with other ecumenical agencies, such as the Vatican's Commission for Religious Relations with the Jews, in the pursuit of objectives mentioned above. Cooperation should also occur at the local level between congregations and between interchurch agencies.

3) Collect materials that have to do with Lutheran–Jewish relations, and serve as a channel for their distribution. Work has already been done on the development of materials for ministers and congregations. Information has been prepared, for example, which will help pastors approach such texts as those which have been assigned for the 10th Sunday after Trinity (i.e., dealing with the destruction of Jerusalem). Close cooperation in this activity with the Lutheran World Federation and through the Lutheran World Federation with other churches is of highest importance. The Lutheran World Federation can serve as a clearinghouse of information about activities in member churches, studies conducted by theological faculties, educational materials, etc. We urge that theological faculties be regularly informed about such studies. It is important that Lutherans share with each other what they know about developments in this field of interest.

4) Encourage and facilitate the production of good educational materials for practical use on the regional and local levels. We urge the Lutheran World Federation staff to develop a strategy for making contact with educational commissions and publishing houses of the churches.

5) Remind all Lutheran agencies of the importance of consulting with representatives of the Jewish community when statements about Lutheran–Jewish relations are being prepared. Some churches have made, and continue to make, analyses of their literature with reference to explicit or implicit anti-Semitism. We urge those of our member churches that have not done so to begin this task immediately and that, if at all possible, Jews be drawn in as consultants. We also recommend that when Jews are invited to attend conferences as consultants, they be included in the planning stage.

6) Hold occasional conferences for the purpose of facilitating new initiatives in study and action, to give a more adequate expression of a common mind among Lutherans, and to induct new persons into the field of study and work.

7) Take steps to prevent the isolation of Lutheran–Jewish relations from the area of mission in general. We propose that Lutheran–Jewish activities be pursued in concert with the Lutheran World Federation Department of Church Cooperation.

8) Provide suitable staff support for the international coordination of Lutheran efforts to approach Jews in a responsible manner. We are aware of financial problems, but we give such high priority to this work that we urge the establishment of a separate desk or office in the Lutheran World Federation to deal with Lutheran–Jewish relations. We also recommend that a small advisory group be established to work with the Department of Studies staff both in following up the recommendations of this consultation and in planning for additional work in the area of Lutheran-Jewish concerns.

9) Recommend to member churches that in each country or church, where feasible, a central office or desk be established for responsibilities for Lutheran–Jewish concerns similar to those carried by the Lutheran World Federation.

10) Give place to Lutheran–Jewish concerns both in the planning and on the agenda of the 1977 Lutheran World Federation Assembly.

4

Some Observations and Guidelines for Conversations between Lutherans and Jews

INTRODUCTION BY HAROLD H. DITMANSON

At this point in our examination of Lutheran statements, we can turn from the international to the American scene. The first document to claim our attention is rather brief. The executive committee of the Lutheran Council in the U.S.A. requested the division of theological studies to prepare a statement of guidelines for use in Lutheran–Jewish conversations. This document was sent in 1971 to the church bodies participating at that time in the Lutheran Council and in the Lutheran World Federation. The three elements we have been tracking through other statements are present here. The opening and closing paragraphs express in the strongest terms the moral obligation to cooperate in the quest for justice and peace and to oppose all forms of anti-Semitism and discrimination. The traditional theology of replacement is present in a low-key manner in the reference to "the mission of the church" in the second paragraph. But it is qualified by the assertion that the mission "includes conversations, and indeed must often begin with them." The bulk of the statement deals with conversations in such a way as to play down the traditional theology of replacement. The third paragraph, for example, enumerates attitudes that hardly cohere with a "haves" and "have-nots" approach, especially the references to mutual respect and to the willingness to risk confronting real differences. The fifth observation says explicitly that on both sides of the conversation there are "living communities of faith and worship," and that "neither polemics nor conversions are the aim of such conversations." This document points very clearly to a theology of recognition rather than of replacement and thus speaks with a rather different voice from that which is heard in sections I and II of the Løgumkloster report and sections I and II of the Oslo report.

SOME OBSERVATIONS AND GUIDELINES FOR CONVERSATIONS BETWEEN LUTHERANS AND JEWS

This document was prepared by the Division of Theological Studies, Lutheran Council in the U.S.A., at the request of the Council's Executive Committee. It was transmitted in April, 1971, to the church bodies participating in the Lutheran Council: the American Lutheran Church, the Lutheran Church in America, and the Lutheran Church–Missouri Synod.

Improved relationships among separated Christian churches in recent decades have also led to growing conversation between Jewish and Christian groups. We commend all endeavors which seek greater understanding, mutual confidence, elimination of tensions, and cooperation in the quest for justice and peace, and note statements issued by Lutheran groups which are helpful in these areas.

Amid the pluralism of American society today and in the face of many practical problems facing Christians, Jews, and all men of good will, it is especially necessary to foster and expand such conversations on more local levels, as a contribution to community understanding and cooperation, to heal wounds of the past, and to understand better our common heritage and common humanity. Today the mission of the church surely includes such conversations, and indeed must often begin with them. We urge Lutheran pastors, people, and institutions to seek greater involvement in such endeavors.

The Christian cannot fully understand what it means to be Jewish but our common ground in humanity and in the Hebrew Scriptures makes a base for beginning. In order to have authentic relationships there must be honesty, openness, frankness, and mutual respect along with a recognition of the real differences that exist and a willingness to risk confronting these differences. To these ends we offer some practical suggestions and make some observations as to methods so that conversation may be both honest and fruitful.

1. In localities where Lutherans are comparatively few in number, they are encouraged to cooperate with other Christian groups in initiating and sustaining conversation with Jews.

2. Where Lutherans comprise a substantial group within a locality, they are encouraged to take the initiative in fostering conversation and community understanding.

3. Meetings should be jointly planned so as to avoid any suspicion of proselyting and to lessen the danger of offense through lack of sensitivity or accurate information about the other group.

4. Because of the long history of alienation between the two groups, Christians and Jews should remember that one meeting does little more than set the stage for serious conversations. False hopes and superficial optimism by either group can lead to despair and further alienation.

5. On both sides, living communities of faith and worship are involved. Because of fervent commitments emotions may run deep. It should be underscored that neither polemics nor conversions are the aim of such conversations, nor is false irenicism or mere surface agreement. There may remain honest differences, even as broad areas of agreement are discovered.

6. If we have been open and have shared our assumptions, prejudices, traditions, and convictions, we may be able to share in realistic goal setting, especially in regard to further understanding and common cause in spiritual and social concerns such as fostering human rights.

7. Different methods of procedure may be followed as mutually determined locally, such as:

a. Educational visits to advance mutual understanding of artistic, liturgical tradition.

b. Exchange of visits at regular worship services, "open houses," and special celebrations, followed by explanation and discussion.

c. Informal small group discussions in homes in the manner of the "living room dialogues." Participants may involve one synagogue and one congregation or neighborhood group without regard to membership.

d. Weekend retreats with equal participation of members from both groups and equality of expertise.

e. Popular lectures, discussion, and demonstrations by well-informed resource persons. Lutherans might invite representatives of the American Jewish Committee, Jewish Chatauqua Society, Anti-Defamation League of B'nai B'rith, National Conference of Christians and Jews, and Jewish theological schools.

f. Scholarly lectures and discussions by experts in biblical, historical, and theological studies.

8. Possible topics include: Our Common Heritage; The People of God and Covenant; Christian and Jewish Views of Man; The Significance of Hebrew Scriptures Today; Law, Righteousness, and Justice; State of Israel; The Christian Church in Israel; Survey of the Attitudes and Teachings of

the Church Concerning Judaism; The Image of the Jew in Christian Literature; Luther and the Jews; The Meaning of Suffering; Can a Hebrew Christian be a Jew? An Israeli?; Eschatology in Christian and Jewish Theology; The Significance of the Septuagint; The Universal God in an Age of Pluralism; The State and the Religious Community in Jewish and Lutheran Traditions; What Can We Do Together?

9. Christians should make it clear that there is no biblical or theological basis for anti-Semitism. Supposed theological or biblical bases for anti-Semitism are to be examined and repudiated. Conscious or unconscious manifestation of discrimination are to be opposed.

5

The American Lutheran Church and the Jewish Community

INTRODUCTION BY HAROLD H. DITMANSON

In 1973, Dr. David W. Preus, president of the American Lutheran Church, sent a letter to Dr. Ronald M. Hals, Dr. Edwin A. Schick, Rev. Roderick D. Olson, and to me. He explained that at the 1972 General Convention of The American Lutheran Church, a resolution was adopted asking that the general president appoint a special committee to prepare a statement about the relationship of American Lutherans to Jews. "It seems apparent to many," he wrote, "that we need a clear statement of our relationship with the Jewish community and our intentions." The persons named were asked to serve on the special committee and I was asked to function as chairman and convener.

As a committee we had a free hand and were of a common mind. We agreed on the structure of the report and each member accepted a writing assignment. Roderick Olson wrote section I, Ronald Hals wrote section II, and I wrote section III and the preamble. Edwin Schick, who had health problems during those weeks, drafted the covering letter that went to the church council of The American Lutheran Church. I had editorial responsibility for the final draft.

The preamble was written with memories of the Jewish–Lutheran colloquia held in 1969, 1970, 1971, and 1973 fresh in my mind. The content of the preamble belongs chiefly to the level of moral obligation and exhortation. The deicide charge is rejected, Christian guilt is acknowledged, and joint efforts on behalf of a more humane society are urged. There are, however, a few theological nuances of the revisionist type. For example, it is affirmed that Jews and Christians worship the same God and that Jewish worship is genuine worship, not empty ritual. The preamble also declares that Lutherans must learn theological lessons from the holocaust.

Chapter I contains several themes that point to an approach that differs from that found in Løgumkloster I and II and Oslo I and II. It is said that Judaism is a living and growing religion and that Lutherans should ask Jews to tell them about the development of postbiblical Judaism.

The section entitled "Our Spiritual Solidarity" breaks new ground in Lutheran statements. The thorough Jewishness of early Christianity is emphasized. It is repeated that Judaism and Christianity worship the same God and are both covenant communities. These ideas are consistent with a theology of recognition but hardly fit with a theology of replacement. The hope is expressed that the recognition of solidarity will serve to reduce anti-Jewish prejudice by showing that the two communities stand together rather than over against each other. It is important here that the moral imperative to act humanely does not operate on its own alongside a theology of replacement. We are reminded at this point of the discovery by Glock and Stark (*Christian Beliefs and Anti-Semitism*, 1966) that Christian perceptions of the theological otherness and apartness of Jews generated anti-Jewish attitudes and actions. Thus the emphasis here is on what Judaism and Christianity have in common. The common heritage is prior to the differences in both theological and practical respects. Our first obligation to our Jewish neighbors is to listen and learn from them, rather than to instruct them about God as though they are outsiders and we are insiders.

Chapter II attempts to face the differences between the communities of faith. I would like to say, with a certain amount of what Reinhold Niebuhr called "sinful pride," that this text is the most satisfactory statement on the subject to be found in any Lutheran document. Ronald Hals drafted this chapter but each member of the committee had something to say about it. We determined to make the statement as strong as we could within the limits of a readable and discussable convention report. It was our judgment that the factors that inhibited Lutherans from naming Luther and repudiating his anti-Semitic writings at Løgumkloster did not operate in our situation. The acceptance of the entire report by The American Lutheran Church at its general convention in 1974 vindicated the committee's belief that the church was mature enough to acknowledge and assimilate data that could be threatening to holders of the classic theology of replacement. Everything said in other Lutheran statements about Christian and Lutheran wrongdoing is included here, but amplified and strengthened. It was our hope that Jewish readers would see here a sincere effort to be honest and repentant without any note of self-justification.

About the section entitled "Distinctive Ideas, Doctrines, and Practices," I will only say that in clarifying such notions as denomination, Jewishness, Jewish theology, Jewish practices, and biblical authority, the document is asking Lutherans to abandon the stereotypes that have always been a part of the theology of replacement and to allow Jewishness and Judaism to be defined by Jews. It is clear that Christians both agree and disagree with the tenets of Jewish religion. We worship the same God but disagree about Jesus Christ. The disagreements, however, are to be seen as the doorway to a dialogue in which the appropriate importance of the difference can be estimated, not just taken for granted, and out of which mutual understanding may emerge.

Chapter III bears a strong resemblance to section II of the Neuendettelsau report issued a year earlier. I had written the paragraphs in the Neuendettelsau document (II,F) which dealt with social cooperation, witness, dialogue, and education. I had not changed my mind about these topics during the intervening year and thought in fact that it would be a positive move if The American Lutheran Church were to reaffirm as its own declaration something of what the Lutheran World Federation had said on these topics. I was also quite sure that the understanding of mission and dialogue set forth in the Neuendettelsau report was the only fair and effective way of presenting that controversial topic to the convention of The American Lutheran Church.

Therefore the whole topic of witness is again addressed under the heading of the "sharing of convictions." It is frankly admitted that Lutherans do not agree on this issue. The committee thought that such an admission was honest and realistic and that all of us should learn to live with it. The admission and enumeration of divergent positions was also a breakthrough of some kind since most church documents strive mightily to present a unified point of view. Despite the good intentions behind such efforts, many of us know that consensus does not actually exist and that honest differences of opinion within the church are frequently covered over by the impression of unanimity. Therefore the report states that some Lutherans promote mission on the basis of a theology of replacement while others draw away from special missions to Jews on the basis of a theology of recognition or of some version of a "two-covenant" theory. This approach implied that The American Lutheran Church was strong enough to accommodate divergent theologies of Jewish–Christian relations. Therefore under the rubric of witness as sharing, some will pursue mission and others will pursue dialogue.

A definite move was made to incorporate the Lutheran Council "Observations and Guidelines" of the previous year into the official records and directives of The American Lutheran Church. Since it was obvious that the Lutheran Council document leaned toward dialogue and a theology of recognition, the final sentence to the effect that the dialogical approach "does not rule out mission" was inserted in order to be fair to those who would disagree with the approach of the drafting committee and who ought to be able, in a free country and a free church, to act according to their own convictions.

The concluding paragraphs on "The State of Israel" take seriously the point that this topic cannot be avoided in Jewish–Lutheran conversations. The statement is an attempt to be concrete, honest, and fair with respect to the different points of view within the constituency of The American Lutheran Church.

THE AMERICAN LUTHERAN CHURCH AND THE JEWISH COMMUNITY

This excerpt is from *1974 Reports and Actions, Part 3, Seventh General Convention of The American Lutheran Church*, pp. 917-922.

Preamble

There are many cogent reasons which urge us to reconsider the relationship of Lutherans, and indeed of all Christians, to Jews. Christians are not as aware as they should be of the common roots and origin of the church and the Jewish tradition of faith and life. Both Judaism and Christianity regard the Hebrew Bible—the Old Testament—as the document which bears witness to the beginning of God's saving work in history. They worship the same God and hold many ethical concerns in common, even though they are divided with respect to faith in Jesus of Nazareth as the Messiah.

Christians must also become aware of that history in which they have deeply alienated the Jews. It is undeniable that Christian people have both initiated and acquiesced in persecution. Whole generations of Christians have looked with contempt upon this people who were condemned to remain wanderers on the earth on the false charge of deicide. Christians ought to acknowledge with repentance and sorrow their part in this tragic history of estrangement. Since anti-Jewish prejudice is still alive in many parts of the world, Christians need to develop a sympathetic understanding of the renewal among Jews of the terror of the Holocaust. It is as if the numbness of the injury has worn off, old wounds have been reopened, and Jews live in dread of another disaster. Christians must join with Jews in the effort to understand the theological and moral significance of what happened in the Holocaust.

We need also to look to the future to see if there are things Christians and Jews can do together in service to the community. Better communication between Christians and Jews can lead to more adequate joint efforts on behalf of a humane society. The new atmosphere in theological research and interfaith encounter which has developed within recent years summons us to undertake serious conversations with Jewish people. Some Christians feel a special concern to explore the contribution which American churches might make in and through contacts with their Jewish neighbors and others to a resolution of the conflict in the Middle East that will be to the benefit of all those living in that region.

The urgency of the foregoing considerations is heightened by the fact that about 50 percent of all Jews live in North America. As Lutherans we ought, therefore, to regard our Jewish neighbors as major partners in the common life.

We urge that Lutherans should understand that their relationship to the Jewish community is one of solidarity, of confrontation, and of respect and cooperation.

I. SOLIDARITY

Our Common Humanity

Lutherans and Jews, indeed all mankind, are united by virtue of their humanity. Lutherans and Jews agree that all people, regardless of race, religion, or nationality are equally God's children, and equally precious in his sight. This conviction is based on a concept of God as Creator of the universe, who continues to care for his creation, whose mercies are over all his creatures.

Our Common Heritage

The existence of Jewish congregations today shows that a religious tradition which traces its ancestry back to the time of Abraham is still living and growing. It is a tradition that gave rise to Christianity; a tradition from which Christianity has borrowed much. But modern Judaism has grown, changed, and developed considerably beyond the Judaism of biblical times, just as the modern church has grown, changed, and developed considerably beyond its New Testament beginnings.

It is unfortunate that so few Christians have studied Judaism as it grew and flowered in the centuries since the New Testament era. The first step for Lutherans, therefore, is to devote themselves to completing this long-neglected homework. It is strongly recommended that Lutherans ask the Jews themselves to teach them about this long and critically important period in Jewish history.

Our Spiritual Solidarity

Our solidarity is based on those ideas and themes held in common, most of which were inherited by Christianity from the Jewish tradition. It is important to note that the ministry of Jesus and the life of the early Christian community were thoroughly rooted in the Judaism of their day. To emphasize the Jewishness of Jesus and his disciples, and to stress all that binds Jews and Christians together in their mutual history, is also to attack one of the sources of anti-Jewish prejudice. We are, after all, brothers one to another. Judaism and Christianity both worship the one God. We both call Abraham father. We both view ourselves as communities covenanted to God. We both feel called to serve in the world as God's witnesses and to be a blessing to mankind.

This emphasis on solidarity is not meant to ignore the many differences that exist between Lutherans and Jews. Rather it is through an understanding and appreciation of what we have in common that we can best discuss our differences. But for the moment, Lutherans have an obligation to fulfill— namely, to understand adequately and fairly the Jews and Judaism. This is the immediate purpose of Lutheran conversations with Jews.

It is hoped that as Lutherans better understand this similar, yet different religious tradition, the wounds of the past will be healed, and Lutherans and Jews together will be able to face the future receptive to the direction of the Holy Spirit as he seeks to accomplish the will of the One in whom all men live and move and have their being.

II. CONFRONTATION

The History of Separation and Persecution

American Lutherans are the heirs of a long history of prejudicial discrimination against Jews, going back to pre-Christian times. The beginnings of this history of hate are obscure, but gross superstition and the desire for a scapegoat were prominent aspects. The separation between church and synagogue became final by the end of the first century. When Christianity was made the official religion of the Roman Empire, a systematic degradation of Jews began in which both church and empire played their parts. Jews were regarded as enemies who were to be eliminated by defamation, extermination, prohibition of their writings, destruction of their synagogues, and exclusion into ghettos and despised occupations. During these 19 centuries, Judaism and Christianity never talked as equals. Disputation and polemics were the media of expression. More recent developments reflect the continuation of patterns of ethnic behavior growing out of this heritage, by which Jews have been excluded by non-Jews, and have, in turn, themselves drawn together in separate communities.

No Christian can exempt himself from involvement in the guilt of Christendom. But Lutherans bear a special responsibility for this tragic history of persecution, because the Nazi movement found a climate of hatred already in existence. The kindness of Scandinavian Lutherans toward Jews cannot alter the ugly facts of forced labor and concentration camps in Hitler's Germany. That the Nazi period fostered a revival of Luther's own medieval hostility toward Jews, as expressed in pugnacious writings, is a special cause of regret. Those who study and admire Luther should acknowledge unequivocally that his anti-Jewish writings are beyond any defense.

In America, Lutherans have been late and lethargic in the struggle for minority rights in the face of inherited patterns of prejudice. We have also been characterized by an inadequate level of ethical sensitivity and action in social and political areas.

Distinctive Ideas, Doctrines, Practices

Customarily, American Lutherans have increased misunderstanding by trying to picture Jews as a "denomination" or "faith-community" like themselves. Actually, Jewishness is both a religious phenomenon and a cultural phenomenon which is exceedingly hard to define. While for most Jews, ancient and modern, it is seen as a matter of physical descent, the aspects of religion and nationhood have at times occupied decisive positions, as is currently true in regard to Zionism. We create misunderstanding when we persist in speaking of "Jewish" creeds and "Jewish" theology, for not all Jews necessarily believe in Judaism, although that religion is their heritage.

Judaism, while it does indeed have teachings, differs markedly from Christian denominations in that its essence is best summed up not in a set of beliefs or creeds, but in a way of life. The distinctive characteristics of the words "Jew" and "Judaism" should neither be ignored nor should they be revised to fit better with Christian presuppositions. We must rather allow Jewishness to be defined by Jews, and content ourselves with the already tremendous difficulties of trying to keep aware of the complexities of this shifting and not uncontradictory self-understanding.

To the extent that both religious practices and theological reflection manifest themselves among Jews, some basic guidelines can be attempted. There is no reason why Jewish practices and beliefs should be understood or judged differently from those of any minority group. They ought, indeed, to be respected especially by Christians, since they flow from a tradition which served as the "mother" of Christianity. But even where they are in disagreement with the practices and beliefs of Christians, they still deserve the same full protection and support which are given to the religious convictions of any American citizen. While modern interest in ethnicity has furthered the appreciation of diversity of heritages, American Lutherans still need warnings against bigotry and urgings to work toward minority rights.

The unique situation of the sharing of the books of the Hebrew Scriptures by Lutherans and Jews is the source of great problems as well as the potential for significant dialogue. Because Jews are not a "denomination" with a unity shaped by a theological consensus, these Scriptures do not have the same role for them as they do for us. For both Jews and Lutherans the Old Testament has a kind of mediate authority. For Jews this authority is mediated by millennia of tradition and by the individual's choice as to whether or not he will be "religious." For Lutherans as well, the Hebrew Scriptures do not have independent authority. They gain their significance from their role as *Old* Testament and are subordinated to the New Testament Christ, in whom they find a complex fulfillment, involving cancellation as well as acceptance, and reinterpretation as well as reaffirmation. Lutherans must affirm what Jews are free to accept or reject, namely, that it is the same God who reveals himself in both Scriptures. The consequence of this is that Lutherans must view Judaism as a religion with which we in part agree wholeheartedly and yet in part disagree emphatically. Judaism worships the same God as we do (the God of Abraham is our God), yet it disavows the Christ in whom, according to Christian faith, all God's promises have their fulfillment and through whom God has revealed the fullness of his grace.

71

In view of these divergences, Lutherans and Jews will differ, sometimes drastically, about questions of biblical interpretation, especially in regard to Christian claims about the fulfillment of the Old Testament. Such disagreements should not be the cause of either anger or despair, but rather should be seen as the doorway to a dialogue in which there can occur the discovery of both the real sources of the divergences and their appropriate degree of importance. Out of such learning there can come a mutuality of understanding which can make witness far more meaningful.

III. RESPECT AND COOPERATION

In recognition of the solidarity that unites us and of the tensions and disagreements which have divided us, we affirm the desire of The American Lutheran Church to foster a relationship of respect and cooperation with our Jewish neighbors.

Cooperation in Social Concern

Jews and Lutherans live together in the same society. They have common problems and obligations. The bonds of common citizenship ought to impel Lutherans to take the initiative in promoting friendly relationships and in making common cause with Jews in matters of civic and social concern. It is of special importance that Lutherans demonstrate their commitment to the intrinsic worth of Jewish people by giving them all possible assistance in the struggle against prejudice, discrimination, and persecution. Jews and Lutherans need not share a common creed in order to cooperate to the fullest extent in fostering human rights.

A Mutual Sharing of Faith

Within a context of respect and cooperation, Lutherans should invite Jews to engage in a mutual sharing of convictions. Lutherans who are aware of the Jewish roots of their faith will be moved by both a sense of indebtedness and a desire for deeper understanding to share on the level of religious commitment. Many Lutherans wish to engage in a mutual sharing of convictions, not only for the sake of greater maturity, but also because Christian faith is marked by the impulse to bear witness through word and deed to the grace of God in Jesus Christ.

It is unrealistic to expect that Lutherans will think alike or speak with one voice on the motive and method of bearing witness to their Jewish neighbors. Some Lutherans find in Scripture clear directives to bear missionary witness in which conversion is hoped for. Others hold that when Scripture speaks about the relation between Jews and Christians its central theme is that God's promises to Israel have not been abrogated. The one approach desires to bring Jews into the body of Christ, while the other tends to see the church and the Jewish people as together forming the one people of God, separated from one another for the time being, yet with the promise that they will ultimately become one.

It would be too simple to apply the labels "mission" and "dialogue" to these points of view, although in practice some will want to bear explicit witness through individuals, special societies, or ecclesiastical channels, while others will want to explore the new possibilities of interfaith dialogue. Witness, whether it be called "mission" or "dialogue," includes a desire both to know and to be known more fully. Such witness is intended as a positive, not a negative act. When we speak of a mutual sharing of faith, we are not endorsing a religious syncretism. But we understand that when Lutherans and Jews speak to each other about matters of faith, there will be an exchange which calls for openness, honesty, and mutual respect. One cannot reveal his faith to another without recognizing the real differences that exist and being willing to take the risk of confronting these differences.

We wish to stress the importance of interfaith dialogue as a rich opportunity for growth in mutual understanding and for a new grasp of our common potentiality for service to humanity. We commend to The American Lutheran Church the LCUSA document, "Some Observations and Guidelines for Conversations between Lutherans and Jews," as a helpful means toward realizing the goals of interfaith dialogue. It should be understood that the LCUSA document limits itself to the aims and methods of dialogue and does not attempt to cover the entire field of Lutheran–Jewish relationships. Consequently, its comment that "neither polemics nor conversions are the aim of such conversations" does not rule out mission.

The State of Israel

The LCUSA "Guidelines" wisely suggest that "the State of Israel" be one of the topics for Jewish–Lutheran conversations. The tragic encounter of two peoples in the Middle East places a heavy responsibility upon

Lutherans to be concerned about the legitimacy of the Jewish state, the rights of the Palestinians, and the problems of all refugees.

The history and circumstances of the Israeli–Arab conflict are very complicated. It is understandable that Lutherans should be deeply divided in their evaluation of the situation in the Middle East. In Jewish opinion, Israel is more than another nation. It is a symbol of resurrection following upon the near extinction of the Jewish people within living memory. There are also some Lutherans who find a religious significance in the State of Israel, seeing in recent events a fulfillment of biblical promises. Other Lutherans espouse not a "theology of the land," but a "theology of the poor," with special reference to the plight of the Palestinian refugees. Still other Lutherans endorse what might be called a "theology of human survival," believing that the validity of the State of Israel rests on judicial and moral grounds.

It seems clear that there is no consensus among Lutherans with respect to the relation between the "chosen people" and the territory comprising the present State of Israel. But there should be a consensus with respect to our obligation to appreciate, in a spirit of repentance for past misdeeds and silences, the factors which gave birth to the State of Israel and to give prayerful attention to the circumstances that bear on the search for Jewish and Arab security and dignity in the Middle East.

6

To Share Gospel with Jews

To Encourage Evangelism among the Jews

A Statement of Jewish–Lutheran Concerns

INTRODUCTION BY HAROLD H. DITMANSON

The three statements in this section express the mind and will of the 52nd Regular Convention of The Lutheran Church–Missouri Synod (1977). I cannot comment on any factors that lie behind these documents since I had no part in their production. The Overture, "To Share Gospel with Jews," affirms the universal need of salvation through Jesus Christ and notes that the Lutheran Church–Missouri Synod has "too often bypassed the Jews in evangelism." Such neglect is described as one of "the worst forms of lovelessness, discrimination, and anti-Semitism." The first resolution expresses gratitude to the Jews for the part they have played in the history of salvation. The second resolution expresses repentance for anti-Semitic actions and attitudes of the past. The rest of the statement is a straightforward expression of the historic Christian position—a program of mission based on a theology of replacement. It is said that because the Jews are sinful people who have been redeemed by Christ, and because they do not know about the gospel, therefore Lutherans should proclaim the gospel to Jews, as to all other people, so that they may hear the good news of salvation.

Instead of the usual mix of three elements found in varying proportions in other Lutheran statements, the reader finds here only two—the element of moral obligation in the references to anti-Semitism, and the traditional theology of replacement with its corollary evangelistic impulse. There are no traces of a revisionist perspective based on a theology of recognition.

Convention Resolution, "To Encourage Evangelism Among the Jews," does not differ from the Overture in content, but describes the practical steps to be taken in order to activate an extensive program of witnessing to the Jewish people. The 1978 "Statement by the Commission on Witnessing to Jewish People" of the Board for Evangelism has a rather different form and is able to suggest more ideas than the 1977 statements. On the moral level a genuine sensitivity is expressed. This includes (1) a note of repentance with respect to the sufferings of Jews at the hands of Christians, (2) a recognition that witnessing to Jews can have the unintended effect of nurturing anti-Semitic attitudes, probably because such witnessing calls attention to the otherness or over-againstness of the Jewish people in relation to the church, and (3) an admonition to Lutherans to seek to understand their Jewish neighbors and to treat them and their faith in a respectful way.

On the theological level the mystery of Jewish–Christian history is faced in two ways. The opening sentence of the document contains the germ of a revisionist perspective, an idea that other Lutherans have developed at greater length: "We desire to be sensitive to the priority place of the Jews as God's chosen people both in the past . . . and in the present, where God's plans for the Jews continue to unfold." It is not said what these "plans" might be. Other Lutherans have been led by the notion of continuing divine "plans" for the Jews or ongoing contact between Jews and the God whom they worship, to say that Judaism is a real and living religion. It is not clear whether this recognition is implied by the opening sentence.

Whatever the possible implications of the sentence might be, however, they do not modify the thrust of the paragraphs that follow. The rest of the document expresses the other way of facing Jewish–Christian history. None of the positive things that can be said about Jewish history or faith can cancel out the Christian obligation to evangelize them in the name of Christ. But moral sensitivity continues to be expressed in the assertion that Jews are not to be singled out as a special target, but are to be included within the normal parish outreach. Moreover no techniques involving manipulation or disrespect are to be used.

Alongside the moral sensitivity, however, there lies the theological affirmation that Lutherans must not forget the clear and undeniable biblical truth that Jesus is the Messiah, the fulfiller of Old Testament prophecies, and the only way of salvation. We are encouraged to join the apostles in praying and working for the salvation of the Jews. We see here a clear expression of the classic Christian rationale for missions to the Jews, although free of any spirit of antagonism or arrogance. The resolution that outlines the rather intensive and churchwide two-year program of preparation for witnessing to Jews strikes the reader as coming close to singling Jews out for special attention. It is implied that this must be done in order to remedy past neglect. Still, the scale of the enterprise goes far beyond what other Lutherans have wanted to advocate.

To Share Gospel with Jews

Convention Workbook (Reports and Overtures), 52nd Regular Convention, The Lutheran Church–Missouri Synod, Dallas, Texas, July 15–22, 1977. Excerpt, p. 31: 2.08A.

WHEREAS, Approximately six million Jews live in the United States; and

WHEREAS, The vast majority know practically nothing about the New Testament Gospel and not much more about a personal Messiah as promised in the Old Testament and are still without Christ and without hope; and

WHEREAS, The Jews have sinned and come short of the glory of God as well as the Gentiles (Rom. 3:23); and

WHEREAS, The Jews have been redeemed by Christ as well as the Gentiles (1 John 2:2); and

WHEREAS, Salvation for the Jews is by grace through faith in Christ as well as for Gentiles (Rom. 10:11-13); and

WHEREAS, Our Savior commissioned us to baptize and to teach all things He has commanded to the Jews as well as to the Gentiles (Matt. 28:19-20); and

WHEREAS, The Lord has promised to bless His Word wherever it is sown, be it among Jew or Gentile (Rom. 1:16; Is 55:10-13); and

WHEREAS, We of The Lutheran Church–Missouri Synod have too often bypassed the Jews in evangelism visits and in the opening of new mission stations; and

WHEREAS, Bypassing the Jewish people in missions and evangelism is one of the worst forms of lovelessness, discrimination, and anti-Semitism possible; and

WHEREAS, Our Savior Jesus Christ Himself was a Jew and the apostles who were willing to lay down their lives in order that we might hear the Good News of salvation were also Jews; therefore be it

Resolved,

1. That we remind ourselves that salvation came to us through the Jews and recognize the great debt we owe them;

2. That we repent of any anti-Semitic actions, statements, and attitudes of the past;

3. That we repent of our past neglect in evangelizing the Jews and ask the Lord's gracious forgiveness;

4. That we in the future treat the Jews like anyone else who needs forgiveness and salvation, recognizing the glorious truth that when Christ died He died for all and that faith in Christ as Savior is the only way, but the sure way, to an everlasting life for both Jew and Gentile;

5. That we encourage our synodical and district boards of mission and evangelism to remember the Jews in future mission planning and to refrain from bypassing them simply because they are Jews;

6. That we encourage congregational evangelism committees and individual members of our congregations to show the same love for Jews as for others who need Christ, and to refrain from bypassing the Jews as if there were no hope for them or as if Christ loved them less than others;

7. Finally, that we encourage especially those congregations located in or near Jewish communities to reach out to the Jews with the Gospel of Christ in love and boldness and to welcome them into their congregations and fellowship as Christ has welcomed us.

> Divine Savior Lutheran Church
> N. Fond du Lac, Wis.
> Edward Vandermolen, *President*
> Ida Vandermolen, *Secretary*
> Bruce J. Lieske, *Pastor*

To Encourage Evangelism among the Jews

Convention Proceedings, 52nd Regular Convention, The Lutheran Church–Missouri Synod, Dallas, Texas, July 15–22, 1977. Excerpt, p. 122. Resolution 2-27 Report 2-02, Rec.6 (CW, p.27); Overtures 2-08A—B, 10-18 (CW, pp.31, 326).

WHEREAS, God has made from one man all people to live on the earth as a loving family in harmony and reverence before Him as the only true God (Gen. 1:26; Acts 17:26-27); and

WHEREAS, This relationship was broken by the fall of man into sin; and

WHEREAS, Jesus Christ is the Mediator between God and all mankind and the Savior of the world (1 Tim. 2:3-6); and

WHEREAS, Jesus Christ has broken down the wall of hostility between God and man, between man and his fellowman, and thus also between Jews and Gentiles (Eph. 2:14); and

WHEREAS, So many Christians have not been sensitive to opportunities the Lord has given for cultivating creative, positive relationships; and

WHEREAS, We of The Lutheran Church–Missouri Synod have too often not included the Jews in our mission; therefore be it

Resolved, That we adopt a 2-year goal of persuading 50 percent of our congregations to prepare themselves for effective witness to Jewish people by working through the Bible study materials and witness resources prepared by the Committee on Witnessing to Jewish People; and be it further

Resolved, That we direct the Board for Evangelism to give priority to materials and programs for witness to Jewish people; and be it further

Resolved, That we adopt a 2-year goal of 10 District workshops to stimulate interest and equip our members in witnessing to Jewish people; and be it further

Resolved, That we direct the Board for Social Ministry to include among its concerns the problem of anti-Semitism; and be it further

Resolved, That we urge congregations to share with the committee their reactions to the study materials and witness resources prepared by the Committee on Witnessing to Jewish People to aid in further study; and be it finally

Resolved, That we encourage especially those congregations located in or near Jewish communities to reach out to the Jews and share our faith that Jesus of Nazareth is the promised Messiah.

Action: *Adopted (5).*

A STATEMENT OF JEWISH–LUTHERAN CONCERNS

Adopted January, 1978 by The Commission on Witnessing to Jewish People, The Board for Evangelism, The Lutheran Church–Missouri Synod.

I. We desire to be sensitive:

1. To the priority place of the Jews as God's chosen people both in the past, wherein lie roots of our own religious beliefs and practices, and in the present, where God's plans for the Jews continue to unfold.

2. To the unique history of the Jewish people in which they have suffered much injustice and cruelty at the hands of the Christian church and non-Christian gentiles. We deplore and repudiate this most unfortunate history and pray for a new understanding and spirit.

3. To the danger that witnessing to Jewish people can result in misunderstanding and potential nurturing of anti-Semitic attitudes.

II. We plead for understanding:

1. That we are not singling out the Jewish people as a special target for our evangelistic endeavors. We are committed to a parish approach in which the local congregation is committed to share the Gospel with all people in its community, Jew and Gentile alike. In the past, we have often bypassed some segments of the community, such as the Jewish people.

2. That we are not mounting a campaign to convert Jewish people with techniques of evangelism which involve manipulation, pressure, and disrespect of the individual. Unfortunately, most of our people are not aware of the past injustices. Therefore, we seek to help our congregations understand the contemporary Jewish people who live with them in the community and share their faith with them in a sensitive and respectful way. We need to provide special helps for this purpose just as we do for other groups of people such as blacks, Hispanics, Indians, cults, etc. We have full-time pastors to deaf, Estonians, Puerto Ricans, etc.

III. We state our commitment:

1. That Jesus of Nazareth is the promised Messiah, who fulfilled the prophecies of the Old Testament and by His life, death, and resurrection provided complete atonement for the sins of all people, Jew and Gentile alike.

2. That since the New Testament as well as the Old Testament is the verbally inspired Word of God the words of Jesus remain true for us today: "I am the Way, the Truth, and the Life, no man comes to the Father but by Me" (John 14:6); as do the words of Peter: "There is salvation in no one else, for there is no other name [than the name of Jesus] under heaven given among men by which we must be saved" (Acts 4:12).

3. That we are obligated to share the Gospel of Jesus as Lord and Savior with all people, Jew and Gentile alike (Matt. 28:18-20, Luke 24:46-49), and we seek to follow the example of our Lord and the early apostles with the zeal expressed by St. Paul when he said, "My heart's desire and prayer to God for them [Jews] is that they may be saved" (Rom. 10:1).

4. That we do love the Jewish people, that we stand with them in opposing all forms of anti-Semitism and injustice, that we join them in humanitarian concerns, and will continue to love them even when they choose not to accept our witness.

7

The Significance of Judaism for the Life and Mission of the Church

"The Bossey Report"

INTRODUCTION BY HAROLD H. DITMANSON

The ninth document in this collection of Lutheran statements is the report of the fourth international consultation on the Church and the Jewish People, convened by the department of studies of the Lutheran World Federation. The meeting was held in Bossey, Switzerland, during August, 1982, and is in the line of the Løgumkloster, Neuendettelsau, and Oslo consultations. About 50 persons were invited from 25 countries. Three Jewish guests were present. I was not involved in the Bossey consultation, nor have I had a chance to discuss the dynamics of the meeting with those who took part. As a veteran reader of conference documents, however, I will make some comments about what I see in the text.

At the risk of tampering with the flow of the argument, I am going to track the three elements we have found in other statements: the moral imperative, the traditional theology of replacement, and certain nontraditional or revisionist themes. The moral component is strong in the first and last chapters. Chapter I is entitled, "Christian–Jewish Estrangement." In this section we find an explicit and extended acknowledgment of Christian responsibility for anti-Judaism and anti-Semitism. Lutherans, it is said, have a special problem that must be confronted during the year of Martin Luther's 500th anniversary. "In his later years," the text says, "he made certain vitriolic statements about the Jews that Lutheran churches today universally reject." Lutherans are warned against "the tradition of an anti-Jewish reading of the Bible" because this tradition has negative effects on both Jews and Christians. Throughout the chapter there is an emphasis on the necessity of recovering the solidly Judaic core of Christian faith and worship. The first chapter comes to a conclusion with these words: "We understand the hesitation on the part of some Jews to enter into closer relationship with Christians because of all that has happened in the past, but we hope and pray for a gradual rebuilding of a climate of mutual trust and solidarity between Christians and Jews."

Chapter V, entitled "Tasks for the Future," acknowledges that Christian teaching, preaching, and worship have not presented an adequate picture of Jews and Judaism. A thorough examination of liturgies, lectionaries, hymnbooks, and seminary and church-school instructional materials is recommended, and the *Ten Points of Seelisberg* (1947) are included in an appendix to serve as guidelines. The lessons which Western Christians have learned about their own failures in interfaith relationships should be shared with the churches of Africa and Asia. Through their official publications and in congregational training programs, the churches should help lay people to develop a sense of solidarity with their Jewish neighbors and a willingness to cooperate with them in an effort to bring about a society free of prejudice and discrimination.

I suspect the assembly was of one mind as it expressed the moral and humanitarian obligations outlined in chapters I and V. But, as is the case with almost all such declarations, the line of thought becomes less clear when the theological topics of Christian self-understanding and the continuing role of Judaism come up for discussion. Signs of compromise between traditional and revisionist theologies are evident in chapters II, III, and IV.

Chapter II speaks of the Old Testament as "common ground for Jews and Christians." A reader wonders just how "common" that ground is as the text goes on to assert that "Jews and Christians differ fundamentally in their understanding of it." Apart from the insensitive references to the "Old Testament" and the many definitions of Jewish belief and practice written by Lutherans, not Jews, this chapter, and indeed the entire report, consists of descriptive, balanced, friendly statements. But the traditional notion that the Hebrew Bible is merely preparatory to the apostolic writings is the dominant theme. A minor theme appears in the final paragraph, where one reads: "Christians should realize that this Jewish understanding is not necessarily legalistic but may lead to a life in the presence of God full of spiritual energy." I would like to see this sentence as at least a weak recognition of the reality, validity, or integrity of Judaism before God, since it is said that Judaism can be "a life in the presence of God," rather than the futile exercises of a defective or fossil religion. If I am correct in this view, then the last paragraph is simply inconsistent with the merely instrumental value assigned to Judaism in the preceding paragraphs. If that is the case, one gets a picture of opposing school of thought struggling to gain control of the text, with the traditional theology of replacement getting the lion's share of the space.

This is also the case with chapter III, entitled "Salvation and Faithfulness." It is announced that Jews emphasize faithfulness, while Christians emphasize salvation. Several paragraphs comment on characteristic terms and concepts used by Jews and Christians when they speak about the human will, sin, and vocation. I do not know whether the definitions in this chapter would be regarded as acceptable by representatives of Judaism. The contrast is drawn, however, between the Jewish concept of religion as living out the commands given in the Torah, and the Christian concept of religion as faith or trust in the gracious promises of God. It is said that Christians can learn much from Jews about obedience in daily life, while Jews can learn from Christians the central importance of a gracious God. Although the language is respectful and the contrasts are mildly stated, it is difficult to escape the impression that the old stereotype of Judaism as a religion of law and Christianity as a religion of grace is at work. Whenever it is said that Christianity is more comprehensive because it includes both faith and obedience, whereas Judaism is essentially a moral program with divine backing, the old contrast between that which is partial and that which is complete is there to support the traditional Christian triumphalism. The odd thing is that in the opening lines of this chapter, the text says that these differences between Jews and Christians "are emphases rather than clear distinctions." I have to believe that this sentence, which undermines the rest of the chapter, represents the effort of some revisionist theologians to get a word in edgewise.

Chapter IV, "Sent for the Life of the World," is a very clear and moderate discussion of two different understandings of the calling of the people of God. Judaism sees its vocation as "the radiation of God's presence in the world," whereas the church sees itself as "sent forth to proclaim the Gospel in word and deed." Traditionalist and revisionist themes balance each other out. The "sending" of Christians is consistent with the conviction that "salvation in Christ is an action of God embracing all humankind." This sounds like a theology of replacement and a justification for mission. On the other hand, the chapter says in another paragraph: "In its self-identification, the church is continuously confronted with the mystery of the Jews, who being outside of the church still are God's beloved because of the irrevocable covenant and election (Rom. 11:28-32)." The "unbroken bond" between God and Israel does not harmonize easily with the claim that "salvation in Christ is an action of God embracing all humankind." It appears to me that chapter IV first affirms and then denies that Judaism has salvific significance.

In doing so, this section of the Bossey report is a fair sample of almost all Lutheran declarations since 1964. On the moral level, the apology is sincere and the commitment is very firm. On the theological level, Lutherans cannot make up their group mind. Two perspectives struggle, and take turns playing major and minor roles in public statements. Lutherans, of course, are not original in this respect.

THE SIGNIFICANCE OF JUDAISM FOR THE LIFE AND MISSION OF THE CHURCH

Report of the Consultation

The following Report, having been prepared, discussed, amended and accepted by the Consultation as expression of its common mind, is presented (1) to the Commission on Studies, (2) to other instances of the Lutheran World Federation, and (3) to its member churches for study and appropriate action.

I: Christian–Jewish Entrangement

Christian–Jewish relations today are burdened by a long history of suffering that has been brought upon Jews by the Christian West. Sociological, psychological, and political factors contributed to this burden, but Christians must acknowledge that a decisive influence came from their own religious community. Jesus and the first Christians were Jews, but as early as in the first decades conflict arose because of the proclamation of Jesus as Messiah and Lord. As the Christian church grew beyond its Jewish setting, Christian anti-Judaism developed and was followed many centuries later by ideological anti-Semitism with its disastrous consequences under the Nazi regime.

We Christians today must purge ourselves of any hatred of the Jews and any sort of teaching of contempt for Judaism. In seeking to achieve these goals we need to take into account that anti-Judaism and anti-Semitism did not penetrate all parts of Christianity in the same way and to the same extent. These evils have been much more prevalent in the West than elsewhere.

Lutherans have a special problem: Next year we will celebrate Martin Luther's 500th birthday. In his later years he made certain vitriolic statements about the Jews that Lutheran churches today universally reject. We regret the way in which what Luther wrote has been used to further anti-Semitism. This matter will be the subject of considerable attention during the coming year.

We found it helpful to distinguish between different kinds of Christian–Jewish relations, and between their manifestations in different geographical regions. In discussing relations between *Christians and the Jewish people in general*, we found a wide variety of attitudes, ranging from estrangement or hostility in many Western countries and, to some extent, in pre-war Japan, to feelings of closeness or even kinship to Jews among Christians elsewhere in Asia and Africa.

Relations between *individual Christians and Jews* are a normal feature of life in Israel, in the USA, and in many other Western countries. Acquaintance with Jews provides opportunity for positive relationships although at the same time it permits the effects of estrangement to continue. In countries where there are no Jews, as in many countries of Africa and Asia, neither the problem of estrangement nor the possibility for positive contact is likely to arise.

The attitudes of *Christians toward the state of Israel* may reflect in part the positive or negative policy of the government under which Christians live. Those countries that support the state of Israel may dispose Christians to similar attitudes. Those countries that have no ties to Israel or that have broken diplomatic relations with it may create a negative attitude toward Israel in the minds of their citizens. The frequent identification of Jews in South Africa with the policy of the government there severely complicates the question of Israel for Black Christians in South Africa.

The tradition of an anti-Jewish reading of the Bible has had a negative effect on the *relations between Christians and their Jewish heritage* although the presence of this tradition varies in the different countries represented at this consultation. All of us have been impoverished by an understanding of the Bible that minimizes our Jewish roots.

We find new vitality in the faith as we rediscover how Jewish the Bible is and recall that Jesus and his disciples were Jews. In this connection the development of communities of Hebrew Christians in Israel is to be noted. These communities confess Christ as Lord and yet maintain a sense of continuity and identification with their Jewish heritage.

A deeper understanding of the many liturgical and other elements of Jewish origin in our faith and life has led us to sense more fully how close our relationship to the Jewish people is. We appreciate the help given to us by Jews in bridging the gap between our communities. We understand the hesitation on the part of some Jews to enter into closer relationship with Christians because of all that has happened in the past, but we hope and pray for a gradual rebuilding of a climate of mutual trust and solidarity between Christians and Jews.

Only when we have eradicated the teaching of contempt and hatred from our practice can we hope to bear witness to the good news of God's love.

II: The Old Testament: Common Ground for Jews and Christians

1. The Hebrew Bible, the Christian Old Testament, is common ground for Jews and Christians although they differ fundamentally in their understanding of it.

For the Jews the core of their Holy Scripture, consisting of the Torah (Pentateuch), the Prophets and the Writings, is the Torah: it is supplemented and interpreted in the "oral Torah" of the rabbinic tradition, embodied mainly in the Mishnah and the Talmud.

The apostles and the early church interpreted this Holy Scripture in a new way. Jesus, his life, teaching, death and resurrection was the heart of their faith. This faith led to a radical reinterpretation of the Hebrew Scriptures (which had still not been collected in an agreed version), Jesus having brought the "new covenant" (cf. 1. Cor. 11:25).

The extensive references in the New Testament to the Old Testament, which focus on the person and ministry of Jesus, emphasize the continuity with the earlier self-revelatory words and deeds of the God of Israel. Only by referring to the Old Testament could the apostles express their confession of Jesus as Messiah/Christos. The new revelatory event of Jesus was interpreted, preached and taught largely through the concepts and institutions of the Old Testament, which gave the New Testament message the background essential for its fullest understanding.

Since the early church regarded Jesus as the fulfillment of God's promises of blessing and salvation, not only for his chosen people Israel but also for the nations, it came to differ from the synagogue in gradually shifting the emphasis from the Torah to the prophetic and other writings of the Bible.

Jesus refers to the Old Testament to explain key terms like "Father" or "Kingdom of Heaven." His words and deeds brought "something greater" (cf. Matt.12:41-42). With the sacrifice on the cross the significance of the Torah was changed (cf. Gal.3:10-14) so that it may be said that Jesus is the end, goal, and fulfillment of the law (cf. Rom.10:4).

2. The Old Testament is indispensable for a full understanding of the significance of the person and ministry of Jesus and for explicating the life of the community of faith. The sacred writings of other peoples do not replace the Old Testament. Yet religious traditions from outside the Judaeo–Christian heritage may at times provide resources to enhance the articulation of the gospel in new contexts, as they have in past periods of church history.

3. We recognize that the work of Jewish Bible scholars in the past and present may enrich our own understanding of the Old Testament. For Jews the Torah, with, according to rabbinic tradition, its 613 commandments, is a record of a covenant between God and his people that is still in force. Every Jew is under obligation to participate actively in this covenant by living according to the will of God as expressed in the Torah. The prophetic and other writings of their Bible have an authority which is subsidiary to the Torah.

Christians should realize that this Jewish understanding is not necessarily legalistic but may lead to a life in the presence of God full of spiritual energy. Those early Christians who came from the Jewish people did not want to be led away from obedience to the Torah as it was fulfilled in Christ. Christians generally should learn that faith in Christ does not preclude but rather includes a fulfillment of the Torah in the love of Christ.

III: Salvation and Faithfulness

Jews put great emphasis on faithfulness whereas our own emphasis is more on salvation. However, these are emphases rather than clear distinctions. Jews speak of salvation (God loved the patriarchs, chose their descendants, and gave them the covenant on Mount Sinai. (cf. Deut. 10:12ff). "Christians strive to be faithful ("that I might be his own and live under him in his kingdom and serve him in everlasting righteousness, innocence, and blessedness"—Explanation of the Second Article in Luther's *Small Catechism*). The following paragraphs comment on characteristic terms and concepts used by Jews and Christians when they speak of salvation and faithfulness.

One of the striking differences between Jews and Christians lies in their understanding of the human will. Jews hold that human beings are created with two inclinations, an inclination for good and an inclination for evil. As sons and daughters of the covenant, Jews are urged to choose life and blessing rather than death and curse (Deut. 30) and to keep the commandments of God. It is presupposed that they have the freedom to make this choice.

Christians, on the other hand, hold that they cannot even believe in Jesus Christ unless the Holy Spirit has called them by the Gospel. Before conversion the human will is in bondage to sin. After conversion believers live in tension between slavery and freedom.

When Jews speak of sin, they refer to multiple acts of commission or omission, violations of individual commands. Christians have a more comprehensive view of sin and see it as a power that enslaves. Individual sins are symptoms of the rule of sin in a person's life.

Jews seek to be faithful to the God of the Covenant, and their calling is to live the commands that have been given in the Torah. The concept of corresponding importance for a Christian is faith, or trust in the gracious promises of God. While faith is a free gift, every believer is freed for faithfulness, a life of obedience and discipleship. Paul has expressed well the paradoxical relationship between faith as gift and faithfulness as task: "Work out your own salvation with fear and trembling for it is God who works in you to know and do his will" (Phil. 2:12-13).

For Jews the covenant given to Moses on Mount Sinai is still the basis for membership in the redeemed people. Christians confess that they have been incorporated into a new covenant people through the merits of Jesus Christ.

Jews underscore the importance of obedience here and now, within the covenant community. Christians speak of past liberation from sin, world, and flesh, but they anticipate and look forward to the completion of salvation when God will be all in all, and sin and death will be no more.

Christians can learn much from Jews about faithful living for God and the neighbor in everyday life in this world. "Faith" too easily becomes escape from vocation and reliance on "cheap grace." A faith without faithfulness is no real faith. We hope that Jews might see through our faith the central importance of a gracious God, who calls, gathers, enlightens, and sanctifies the whole church.

These words are a preliminary attempt to understand and to detect divergent emphases. We are not called to judge each other, but to learn from one another about both salvation and faithfulness.

IV: Sent for the Life of the World

From Jewish teachers we have learned how Judaism stresses that all people are brothers and sisters, equals created in the image of God. At the same time Israel—the children of Abraham—has been set apart and chosen for the sake of humankind. This chosenness, however, is not to be understood as privilege or superiority, but as obligation: through its exemplary and Torah-oriented life Israel is to be a blessing and a light to the world, and is thereby also called to hasten the coming of the Messiah and the redemption of the world. Only by being special and different may Jews fulfill their universal calling.

Gentile Christians believe that through Jesus Christ they are grafted into the root of Israel (Rom.11:17ff). Yet in its self-identification the church is continuously confronted with the mystery of the Jews, who being outside of the church still are God's beloved because of the irrevocable covenant and election (Rom.11:28-32).

The Christian sense of vocation in the world finds itself in remarkable accord with that of Judaism, and the church's self-understanding as "the people of God" and a "nation of priests" seem at this point very appropriate.

Like Israel the church is called for the blessing of all humankind. Like Israel it is called to be "a holy people," in the world, yet separate. Like Israel it is to be leaven in the lump, salt of the earth, a light to the world, testifying to the oneness, the majesty and the mercy of God. Like Israel it is called to suffer in the service of God and the world. In this way a living encounter with Judaism reminds and challenges the church with regard to its calling in the world.

However, whereas Judaism describes the vocation of the people as the radiation of God's presence in the world, the New Testament has a different dynamic of missionary consciousness: the church is sent into the world by its living Lord and in the power of the Holy Spirit. The vocation of the church is therefore not only the radiation of exemplary life, but being sent forth to proclaim the Gospel in word and deed. This consciousness of sentness has expressed itself in the going forth of representatives of the Christian church to all parts of the world since the days of Peter and Paul. "As the Father sent me, so I send you." (John 20:21) This sending reminds us that salvation in Christ is an action of God embracing all humankind.

In the last decades Christian communities outside the Western world have come to feel the need in their encounter with indigenous cultures to free Christian faith and life-style from its Western dress. They also stress that the proclamation of the Gospel and the mission of the church should not imply the imposition of foreign culture upon others. In this respect the Jewish people is of twofold importance to the church. In the encounter with Judaism and the Jewish people the church gains a fuller sense of its own biblical roots, which may be the starting point of the process of contextualization. (cf. the LWF consultation for African and Asian pastors on the Jewish roots of Christian worship, Jerusalem, June 1981). At the same time the Jewish people with its calling and particularity reminds us that there is always the countercultural, alien aspect of the life of God's people the world.

In the same way that encounter with Judaism is significant for the church's "sentness" to the world, so also is the encounter with Jews important to Christians. Dialogue in an atmosphere of mutual respect should be pursued. Such dialogue may transform us with regard to our faith and calling; but it also includes a witness to Jesus Christ on our part.

Hebrew Christians have a special role as a link between the church and the Jewish people. According to rabbinic law, Jews who confess Jesus as Messiah and Lord are considered apostate Jews. For the church, however, the presence of Hebrew Christians in its midst is an antidote to the requirement of former centuries that a Jewish convert abandon his own people and heritage. To the rest of the church the Hebrew Christians are a living reminder of the Jewish roots and heritage of the church. As they seek to contextualize the Gospel within their own people, they may also be of help to Christians in other parts of the world in seeking creative alternatives to Western expressions of worship, life-style and witness.

V: Tasks for the Future

1. Christians and the State of Israel

This consultation did not have on its agenda the question of Christian attitudes concerning the state of Israel. We realize, however, that there is a need for our churches to clarify and evaluate the views which are presently held among us. Therefore we recommend that a special consultation on this complicated question be held in the near future.

In the meantime we urge our churches and our fellow Christians to pray and work for justice, peace and reconciliation in the Middle East.

2. Regaining the Jewish roots of our tradition

We have learned that the worship, teaching and preaching of our churches fail in many respects to present an adequate picture of Jews and Judaism. As Christians become more aware of the Jewish roots of their faith, they should make every effort to give expression to this heritage in all fields of the life and work of the church.

■ We urge the member churches of the LWF to make a fair and correct presentation of Judaism in all their teaching and preaching. *The Ten Points of Seelisberg* (see Appendix I) may serve to alert the churches to areas needing special attention.

■ Our liturgies, hymns and prayerbooks make extensive, but selective, use of the Old Testament. We urge that there be an examination of this selection from a theological perspective.

■ When we use the Bible we must make sure that old prejudices against the Jews are not repeated. In connection with the public reading of certain passages (e.g. "his blood be on us and on our children"), worship leaders may need to provide appropriate commentary on the original context. Materials written to assist with sermon preparation and private Bible study should also deal sensitively with Jews and the Jewish heritage.

■ Unbiased information about the history and persecution of the Jewish people in the postbiblical period, as well as in all subsequent centuries, needs to be included at all levels of the church's educational program. The treatment of Jews and Judaism in all curricular materials needs to be evaluated.

■ Teachers of church dogmatics should relate the Christian faith as contained in the ecumenical creeds to its roots in the faith of Israel and to the continuing significance of this common heritage.

■ Liturgies can be enriched by a better knowledge of Jewish worship and the festivals known from the Bible and contemporary Judaism.

3. Special challenges to the churches in Africa and Asia

Although anti-Judaism and anti-Semitism have not played as important a role in Africa and Asia as in the West, the lessons taught by such prejudice and ideology need to be appropriated also by the African and Asian churches. Positive contacts with Jews and Judaism ought to be part of the future agenda of these churches. To begin to meet these challenges we make the following proposals:

■ We have learned that centuries of anti-Judaism and anti-Semitism were exploited by the political ideology of the Nazi era. Therefore Christians in Africa and Asia need to warn their fellow citizens and church members against the use of religious or political ideologies to justify hatred or acts of oppression and persecution toward any religion or people today.

■ The Christian churches of Africa and Asia should help the societies in which they live to eliminate from textbooks, newspapers, and all other public media ideas that might foster prejudice or discrimination. In their own publications, sermons, and pronouncements the churches will want to set the highest standards for treatment of those with different religious or political views.

■ The churches in Africa and Asia are challenged daily by the presence of living, non-Christian religious. As we have all profited by dialogue with Jews and consultations about Judaism, we propose that the LWF initiate ecumenical consultations to assist the churches of Africa and Asia in evaluating theologically the religions in their contexts. Such consultations should investigate how a pluralistic culture can serve as a resource to the churches and how the Gospel is to be articulated in such a culture.

4. Personal relationships and cooperation between Christians and Jews

In this consultation, as in all previous ones, we have seen that plans and programs for Christian–Jewish conferences at the level of church groups have their place and are important.

Appendix I

The Ten Points

The following statement, drawn up at a meeting of the International Conference of Christians and Jews in 1947, and addressed to the churches, has become known as *The Ten Points of Seelisberg*.

1. Remember that one God speaks to us all through the Old and The New Testaments.
2. Remember that Jesus was born of a Jewish mother of the seed of David and the people of Israel, and that his everlasting love and forgiveness embrace his own people and the world.
3. Remember that the first disciples, the apostles, and the first martyrs were Jews.
4. Remember that the fundamental commandment of Christianity, to love God and one's neighbor, proclaimed already in the Old Testament and confirmed by Jesus, is binding upon both Christians and Jews in all human relationships without exception.
5. Avoid disparaging biblical or postbiblical Judaism with the object of extolling Christianity.
6. Avoid using the word Jews in the exclusive sense of the enemies of Jesus, and the words "the enemies of Jesus" to designate the whole Jewish people.
7. Avoid presenting the passion in such a way as to bring the odium of the killing of Jesus upon Jews alone. In fact, it was not all the Jews alone who were responsible, for the cross which saves us all reveals that it is for the sins of us all that Christ died.
8. Avoid referring to the scriptural curses, or the cry of a raging mob: "His blood be upon us and upon our children," without remembering that this cry should not count against the infinitely more weighty words of our Lord: "Father, forgive them, for they know not what they do."
9. Avoid promoting the superstitious notion that the Jewish people is reprobate, accursed, reserved for a destiny of suffering.

10. Avoid speaking of the Jews as if the first members of the church had not been Jews.

Appendix II

Terminology

In dealing with the theme of this consultation, we found that there are terms generally used in our churches that could be misleading. We urge our churches to reexamine their usage.

■ The common Christian use of the terms "Old Testament" and "New Testament" does not imply that the Old Testament is superseded by the New, although it does sometimes have this connotation. Some Christians therefore prefer to speak of the Old Testament as "Hebrew Scripture/Bible" or "First Testament."

■ The Lutheran hermeneutical principle of distinguishing between Law and Gospel is sometimes applied to identify the Old Testament with Law and the New Testament with Gospel. This usage is obviously unjustifiable.

■ The original meaning of *Torah* in the Old Testament is "instruction, guidance, or teaching." The identification of Torah with the word *law* applies only to certain periods in the biblical tradition.

Conclusion by
Harold H. Ditmanson

Throughout this examination of Lutheran statements on Jewish–Lutheran relations, it has no doubt become clear that my bias is towards a revisionist position. A distinct perspective has informed my commentary, although I hope it has not prevented me from being accurate and fair. The thesis that has gradually taken shape during my 20 years of involvement in Jewish–Lutheran relations is that full recognition of the reality of Judaism as a living religion is the essential precondition for any biblically sound, theologically coherent, and humanly fruitful contact between Judaism and Christianity in the future.

It may be naive of me to think that the way is open for such a happy outcome. But consider. All the churches have clearly disavowed the deicide charge. If the deicide charge is rejected because it is false, then it follows that Christians do not think that Jews are the objects of a special form of divine punishment, as though they were a reprobate people. If the Jews are not the objects of a special form of divine punishment, then there is no reason to think that God has abandoned them or cancelled his covenant with them—the form such punishment would take. But if God has not abandoned the Jews, then he must still be with them, in which case their survival, including the practice of their religion, must be due not to God's anger or their own blindness, but to God's gracious, providential design. If this is the case, then Judaism must have a genuine basis of its own in its ongoing covenantal relationship with God. In short, Judaism has a witness God wants it to bear.

Thus the denial of the deicide charge leads straight to the conclusion that Judaism has a reality and autonomy of its own and a positive place in the divine economy. This pattern of thinking strikes me as an organic unity. The rejection of the deicide charge is absolutely fundamental as the first step in all that we do together as Jews and Christians. It stands at one end of the line. But the affirmation of Judaism's covenantal integrity stands at the other end of that line. How a thoughtful Christian can fail to move on to that point, after having affirmed the first point, is very hard for me to understand. Perhaps when God's work with us is finally accomplished, this will be made clear to me, and I will understand even as I am understood.

Additional Documents

Publisher's Note

Harold Ditmanson, noting that the problem of Luther's role in promoting anti-Semitism was treated in different ways in the nine statements, suggested that three additional documents be included in this book.

"Luther, Lutheranism, and the Jews" is a set of three statements written in 1983, the 500th anniversary of Luther's birth. One statement is Jewish, one Lutheran, and one joint.

The papers by Eric Gritsch and Johannes Wallmann explore Luther's anti-Semitic writings, both their historical context in 16th century Europe and their effects in the centuries since then.

8

Luther, Lutheranism, and the Jews

International Jewish Committee on Interreligious Consultation/Lutheran World Federation Dialog, Stockholm, Sweden, 11–13 July 1983.

INTRODUCTORY STATEMENT

A more appropriate but more sensitive subject could scarcely have been chosen for the theme of Jewish–Lutheran conversations in 1983, the five hundredth anniversary of the Reformer's birth, than that of "Luther, Lutheranism, and the Jews."

When the theme was chosen by the small committee that laid plans for a second international Jewish-Lutheran meeting, it was known that it would be difficult. It was not known, however, that in the many events celebrating Luther's birth, this subject would be one of the major points of interest.

The meeting was convened jointly by the Lutheran World Federation and the International Jewish Committee on Interreligious Consultations, the joint agency of five major Jewish organizations (The World Jewish Congress, The Synagogue Council of America, The American Jewish Committee, The B'nai B'rith Anti-Defamation League, and The Jewish Council in Israel for Interreligious Consultations). It was the second of what is expected to be a continuing series of occasions for conversations between representatives of the world Jewish community and the association of Lutheran churches. (The first meeting in Copenhagen in 1981 was devoted to Jewish and Christian teachings on the nature of humankind.)

The group of 12 Jewish and 15 Lutheran participants met in Stockholm on 11–13 July 1983, under the joint chairmanship of Dr. Gerhard Riegner,

Secretary–General of the World Jewish Congress, and Professor Magne Saebo of the Free Faculty of Theology, Oslo.

The aims of the meeting, which was scarcely three days long, could be nothing but simple: to explore the facts and their implications for Jewish–Lutheran relations, and to provide information and encouragement to our constituencies. The program could only be straightforward: two pairs of papers, followed by discussion and the drafting of conclusions. The speakers were: Professor Mark Edwards of Purdue University (USA): Dr. E. L. Ehrlich, Riehen, Switzerland, European Director of B'nai B'rith International: Dr. Ingun Montgomery of Uppsala and Oslo Universities: and Professor Uriel Tal of Tel Aviv University.

That so complex and existential a topic could be dealt with usefully within so short a time could only happen because there were certain favorable conditions: a considerable body of up-to-date literature was available for preparatory study.

Many of the participants were specialists in the subject matter and had indeed participated in earlier events this year, and above all there was a commitment under God to search together for a way to a bridging of the historic gulf of injustice and enmity.

The meeting closed with a brief period of silent prayer for peace in the world and particularly for peace in the Middle East.

The statements that follow are submitted to their readers, Jewish and Christian, in the hope and prayer that they may serve the cause of peace, hope and love between these two communities of believers in one God, and among all humankind.

The LWF delegation was authorized to speak to but not on behalf of the LWF and its constituency. The statements below will be submitted to the appropriate authorities of the LWF for their consideration and action.

JEWISH STATEMENT

On the occasion of the 500th anniversary of the birth of Martin Luther, representatives of the International Jewish Committee on Interreligious Consultations*) (IJCIC) have met for three days in Stockholm with representatives of the Lutheran World Federation to examine the theme: "Luther, Lutheranism, and the Jews."

---

*The international Jewish Committee on Interreligious Consultation (IJCIC) is composed of the World Jewish Congress, the Synagogue Council of America, the American Jewish Committee, the B'nai B'rith Anti-Defamation League, and the Jewish Council in Israel for Interreligious Consultations.

During this year, members of the world Lutheran family have been reviewing the teachings and actions of Luther and their religious, social and political implications. The teachings of Luther have profoundly affected the course of Jewish history, especially in Europe. We are aware of the exploitation of Luther's anti-Judaism by the Nazis to sanction their genocidal campaign against the Jewish people.

In recent years, Lutheran leaders in Germany, Scandinavia, the U.S.A. and elsewhere have made significant efforts to uproot these teachings of contempt that emerged in the writings of Luther in the 16th century. We are heartened by the affirmative direction of the Lutheran–Jewish relationship as manifested in our dialogue in Stockholm.

The Jewish participants welcome the commitment of the Lutheran partners in dialogue to respect the living reality of Judaism from the perspective of Jewish self-understanding and their undertaking that Lutheran writings will never again serve as a source for the teaching of hatred for Judaism and the denigration of the Jewish people. This heralds a new chapter in the relationship between Jews and Lutherans which should find a practical expression in teaching, preaching and worship as well as joint activities for social justice, human rights and the cause of peace.

We pledge ourselves to collaborate with our Lutheran colleagues in facing these common challenges. We trust that this year of Martin Luther observances will thus prove a turning point leading to a constructive future between Lutherans and Jews throughout the world.

JOINT STATEMENT

On the occasion of the 500th anniversary on Luther's birth, representatives of the world Jewish community and world Lutheran community have met in Stockholm July 11–13, 1983, for their second official dialogue.

Meeting in Stockholm, we are mindful of the compassionate response of Scandinavian Christians to the plight of Jewish victims of Nazi persecution forty years ago. This spirit renews our faith in the human capacity to confront evil with courage and determination.

The deliberations on the theme of "Luther, Lutheranism, and the Jews" were informed by an openness of views and a spirit of mutual respect for the integrity and dignity of our faith communities. The discussions revealed a depth of mutual understanding and trust.

1. We affirm the integrity and dignity of our two faith communities and repudiate any organized proselytizing of each other.

2. We pledge to combat all forms of racial and religious prejudice and express our solidarity with all who suffer the denial of full religious freedom.

3. Sharing in the common patrimony of the Prophets of Israel and inspired by their vision, we commit ourselves to strive for a world in which the threat of nuclear warfare will be ended, where poverty and hunger will be eradicated, in which violence and terrorism will be overcome, and a just and lasting peace will be established.

We welcome this historic encounter, which we prayerfully hope will mark a new chapter, with trust replacing suspicion and with reciprocal respect replacing prejudice. To this end, we commit ourselves to periodic consultations and joint activities that will strengthen our common bonds in service to humanity.

LUTHERAN STATEMENT

We Lutherans take our name and much of our understanding of Christianity from Martin Luther. But we cannot accept or condone the violent verbal attacks that the Reformer made against the Jews.

Lutherans and Jews interpret the Hebrew Bible differently. But we believe that a christological reading of the Scriptures does not lead to anti-Judaism, let alone anti-Semitism.

We hold that an honest, historical treatment of Luther's attacks on the Jews takes away from modern anti-Semites the assumption that they may legitimately call on the authority of Luther's name to bless their anti-Semitism. We insist that Luther does not support racial anti-Semitism, nationalistic anti-Semitism and political anti-Semitism. Even the deplorable religious anti-Semitism of the 16th century, to which Luther's attacks made important contribution, is a horrible anachronism when translated to the conditions of the modern world. We recognize with deep regret, however, that Luther has been used to justify such anti-Semitism in the period of national socialism and that his writings lent themselves to such abuse. Although there remain conflicting assumptions, built into the beliefs of Judaism and Christianity, they need not, and should not, lead to the animosity and the violence of Luther's treatment of the Jews. Martin Luther opened up our eyes to a deeper understanding of the Old Testament and showed us the depth of our common inheritance and the roots of our faith.

Yet a frank examination also forces Lutherans and other Christians to confront the anti-Jewish attitudes of their past and present. Many of the anti-Jewish utterances of Luther have to be explained in the light of his polemic against what he regarded as misinterpretations of the Scriptures. He attacked these interpretations, since for him everything now depended on a right understanding of the Word of God.

The sins of Luther's anti-Jewish remarks, the violence of his attacks on the Jews, must be acknowledged with deep distress. And all occasions for similar sin in the present or the future must be removed from our churches.

Hostility toward the Jews began long before Luther and has been a continuing evil after him: The history of the centuries following the Reformation saw in Europe the gradual acceptance of religious pluralism. The church was not always the first to accept this development; yet there have also been examples of leadership by the church in the movement to accept Jews as full fellow citizens and members of society.

Beginning in the last half of the 19th century anti-Semitism increased in Central Europe and at the same time Jewish people were being integrated in society. This brought to the churches, particularly in Germany, an unwanted challenge. Paradoxically the churches honored the people Israel of the Bible but rejected the descendants of those people, myths were perpetuated about the Jews and deprecatory references appeared in Lutheran liturgical and educational material. Luther's doctrine of the Two Kingdoms was used to justify passivity in the face of totalitarian claims. These and other less theological factors contributed to the failures which have been regretted and repeatedly confessed since 1945.

To their credit it is to be said that there were individuals and groups among Lutherans who in defiance of totalitarian power defended their Jewish neighbors, both in Germany and elsewhere.

Lutherans of today refuse to be bound by all of Luther's utterances on the Jews. We hope we have learned from the tragedies of the recent past. We are responsible for seeing that we do not now nor in the future leave any doubt about our position on racial and religious prejudice and that we afford to all the human dignity, freedom and friendship that are the right of all the Father's children.

9

Luther and the Jews: Toward a Judgment of History

Dr. Eric W. Gritsch

The following paper was presented in May, 1983, at one of the Luther Jubilee Year meetings of the Lutheran Council in the USA. There is hardly a more neuralgic topic in Luther research than Luther's attitude to the Jews. Luther's vitriolic outbursts against the Jews have caused pain along the nerves of many Luther scholars as well as various historical bodies connected with the reform movement which bears his name. Lutheranism is particularly afflicted with the neuralgia which links Luther with Hitler, Wittenberg with Auschwitz, and German Protestants with the most vicious anti-Semitism. Yet, whatever the evidence, any judgment regarding the historical Luther must be based on norms established by sound critical methods and an unconditional commitment to judge by substantiated evidence. The evidence of Luther's convictions about the relationship between the Christian gospel and Israel needs to be presented in its historical context; otherwise the full weight of this evidence would be lost.

This paper offers a distillation of research: first it depicts the climate of opinion concerning Jews in Luther's sixteenth-century world; it then presents the Luther position and its interpretation; finally, it proposes a framework for dialogue.

Christian and Jew in the Sixteenth Century

Christian–Jewish relations in the sixteenth century were decisively affected by an enduring anti-Semitism which advocated the segregation of Jews from Christians.[1] Popular medieval Christian propaganda blamed Jews for natural disasters, for the "Black Death" of bubonic plague, and for almost everything else that went wrong in medieval culture and society. In 1348, for example, German Jews were massacred by legal authorities as well as by lynch mobs in Frankfurt, Nuremberg, and Augsburg for poisoning wells, stealing and killing Christian babies, and other crimes conveniently ascribed to Jews as the scapegoats of society. Many Jews were expelled from German cities in the 1480s. Spain, France, and England refused to tolerate Jewish settlements. The Spanish Inquisition of 1492 expelled a quarter million of Jews, who moved along the Mediterranean coast to Italy, Greece, Turkey, Israel, and Persia. Many ended up in a large ghetto in Venice. Some Spanish Jews, known as Marranos, succumbed to sociopolitical pressures and officially converted to Christianity, but continued to adhere to Judaism in secret. The "wandering Jew" quickly became known as a usurer—even though large Christian business corporations practiced a more vicious usury. "Usury" and "Jew" became synonyms, and usurious Christians were called "Christian Jews."

The medieval church supported the segregationist policies of the nations within the Holy Roman Empire. The Fourth Lateran Council of 1215 decreed that Jews were to be distinguished through a yellow patch sown to their clothes. In Germany, Jews were required to wear special hats. Since Jews were known as "Christ killers," stories soon circulated of how they continued to kill Christ in the transubstantiated host. Worship of the eucharistic bread, the *corpus Christi*, was matched by reports of Jewish attacks on the holy host. In 1510, a German pamphlet was circulated in Brandenburg, asserting that Jews had bought and tortured the eucharistic body of Christ. The report described in detail how a Christian citizen had been tempted by the devil to steal the host and its golden container from a Brandenburg church. Afraid of divine punishment, he had sold the host to a wandering Jew named Solomon, who vented his anger against Christ by stabbing the host. At that moment, the holy host turned into three separate parts of Christ. The frightened Jew baked one part of it into Jewish bread. Another part of the host appeared at a Jewish wedding, where guests entertained each other by stabbing Christ's sacramental body. When arrested by the Brandenburg authorities, the Jews admitted having also bought Christian babies and having stabbed them to death. Markgrave Joachim of Brandenburg ordered them to be burned at the stake and confiscated all their possessions. They went to their death with hardened hearts and mocked their Christian executioners. The report added that two Jews converted to Christianity, and 60 remained in Berlin, only to be expelled soon thereafter. Similar stories were reported from other places.[2]

By 1519, most German cities had either expelled the Jews or relegated them to ghetto existence in "Jewish quarters" (*Judenviertel*). On February 21, 1519, the Regensburg city fathers ordered Jews to leave within four days. The chief priest of the city, Balthasar Hubmaier (later known as a leader of the Anabaptists who have survived as Mennonites and Huterites) organized a mob to harass Regensburg Jews whom he labelled "lazy, lecherous, and greedy."[3] After helping to expel Jews, the mob turned against mendicant monks and thus linked their hatred of the Jews to hatred of Roman Catholicism in the name of Luther's Reformation. The written account of the Regensburg mob's activities became a sixteenth-century bestseller. Other bestselling pamphlets accused Jews of witchcraft, blasphemy, and sedition because they violated the laws of Christendom by denying the doctrine of the Trinity and the Virgin Mary. Such nonconformity was viewed as an attack against the foundations of Christian civilization. In 1513, a German edition of a prescription against Jews appeared, known as the "Hammer Against the Jews" (literally, "quiver of arrows of the Catholic faith—*pharetra catholice fide*"), to accompany the prescription against witchcraft issued in 1487 as "Hammer Against Witches" (*malleus maleficarum*). Jews were to be exorcised of their faith and converted to Christianity; theologians condemned them for denying Old Testament prophecies about Jesus.

Even the most tolerant humanists like Erasmus of Rotterdam had no place for Jews in what they perceived to be a Christian world. "All of Erasmus' thought is marked by a virulent anti-Judaism."[4] Erasmus disliked the Jewish religion because of its stress on externals and its legalism; he viewed Christianity as the liberation from a religion of laws, and he considered the Old Testament valid only until the time of Jesus. In such a context he could say that "if hatred of the Jews is proof of true Christianity, then we are all exemplary Christians,"[5] and there can be no toleration of Jews, "the worst plague and the most bitter enemies of Christ's teachings."[6] In short, every stratum of sixteenth-century society considered Jews the diabolical enemies of Christianity and a cancer in society. As Bishop George of Speyer put it on April 4, 1519, when he ordered the total segregation of Jews from Christians in his diocese, "They are not human beings but dogs."[7]

In the face of such hatred, many Jews viewed Luther as a friend since he led a movement against Roman Catholicism and its tyranny. Whereas sixteenth-century Jewish interpretations of the Reformation varied, some significant defenders of Judaism welcomed Luther as God's agent sent to destroy corrupt Rome before the end of the world. The Spanish rabbi Abraham ben Eliezer Halevi advocated the apocalyptic notion that the time had come when God called on the world to repent and to return to the fold of his people, the Jews. Lutheran and humanist interests in the study of Hebrew and the impending schism in the Western church convinced Halevi that the Reformation was the God-sent event that would make Judaism the religion of the end.[8] Other spokesmen of Judaism, such as Rabbi Josel of Rosheim in Germany, did not follow such apocalyptic lines of interpretation. Josel, who had met Luther several times and communicated with other Protestant leaders, was respected by Emperor Charles V and had considerable influence on him. Though not always treated fairly, Josel won enough friends and influenced sufficient people in higher places to avoid the persecution of the small Jewish community in sixteenth-century Germany (only a few hundred Jews were in all of Germany, with the largest community of 78 settled in Frankfurt).[9]

The Luther Evidence

Luther viewed his life and work as being guided by his vocation as biblical scholar. Since, of the 32 years spent on biblical studies, he devoted only three to four years to the study of the New Testament, he has been called "a professor of Old Testament."[10] As such Luther was committed to the classic Christian view maintained for centuries by Christian exegetes that the Old Testament had only one meaning: "to find not only the shadows of the New Testament in the Old Testament, but also to find the direct testimony, indeed, the work of Christ already in the Old Testament."[11] Thus to Luther the Old Testament was a "prefiguration" (*figura*) and "foreshadowing" (*umbra*) of the New Testament, the authors of which are in the "faithful synagogue."[12] Christians, as members of the "faithful synagogue," were to Luther the "spiritual Israel" who continued to trust God's promise to the patriarchs Abraham, Jacob, and Isaac that there will be a "new Israel" in a new world, a new creation brought about by the Messiah. The Old Testament prefigures faith in Jesus Christ, the Messiah born of the seed of Abraham.

The young Luther laid the exegetical foundations for a christological interpretation of the Old Testament already in his first lectures on Psalms from 1513–1515. Following Augustine's differentiation between the "letter" and the "spirit" in the interpretation of the Bible, Luther assumed with Christian hindsight that such passages as Psalm 77:1 ("I cry aloud to God") spoke of a spiritual bondage to sin, death, and evil in the world. The psalmist, therefore, already points to a spiritual Egypt, marked by the yoke of self-righteousness, from which the spiritual exodus of Moses liberated the ancient people of God. Psalms and the Book of Exodus point to a final liberation by the Messiah, Jesus Christ.[13] It took only one further step to argue, as Luther did in his lectures on Romans in 1515, that those Jews who linked spiritual liberation only to themselves as the exclusive people of God were self-righteous. Indeed, God himself "hardened their heart" (Exod. 14:4) so that they, like Pharaoh, would not let the divine promise of salvation go to others. Consequently, when Luther interpreted Paul's declaration that "God shows no partiality" (Rom. 2:11), he depicted Jews as the people who "wanted God to act in such a way that He would bestow the good on the Jews only, and the evil on the Gentiles only"; and he accused the Jews of an idolatrous partiality.[14]

Like many other biblical scholars, Christian and Jewish, Luther viewed his time as the end-time—an apocalyptic age filled with trials and tribulations. The storm and stress of the religious struggle with Rome only confirmed the notion that Christians would be beset, in these last days, by foes from within and without. The pope and the Turks were such foes, according to Luther. But like the first Christians, Luther expected Jews to turn to Christianity, just as Jewish apocalyptic notions expected the nations to assemble in the land of Israel. Zionism and Christian apocalypticism had clashed before, and they clashed again in the sixteenth century. In 1521, Luther advised princes to treat the Jews kindly, because "there are future Christians among them." Luther had the impression that "they were turning every day," trusting in the promise given to them that Christ was the seed of Abraham through whom salvation would come.[15]

Earlier, in 1516, Luther had sided with the Humanist John Reuchlin who, in a famous controversy with a fanatic convert from Judaism, had advocated the study of ancient Hebrew. The convert, John Pfefferkorn, had written crude, polemical tracts against the Jews. Luther's long-time opponent, the Catholic theologian and churchman John Eck, called him a "Jew father" (*Judenvater*).[16] Adherents to the old religion and to the status quo were convinced that Luther's Reformation was synonymous with love for Jews, and that Luther and his followers were the reincarnation, as it were, of these ancient embodiments of hostility to Christianity. At the Diet of Nuremberg in 1522 a rumor was circulated that Luther had denied that Jesus was born of a virgin, and that he considered him merely the son of Joseph. Luther had become a "Judaizer."

Luther's response was quick and to the point in the tract "That Jesus Christ Was Born a Jew" published in 1523. Once again affirming his commitment to the christological interpretation of the Old Testament, Luther nevertheless sided with the Jews who, like him, were being persecuted by the defenders of popish Christendom. The Jews, he contended, are blood-relatives of Christ—"we are aliens and in-laws"; they "are actually nearer to Christ than we are"; and they should be treated kindly.[17] Luther concluded that the Jews do need to be converted, but "not by papal law but by the law of Christian love."

We must receive them cordially, and permit them to trade and work with us, that they may have occasion and opportunity to associate with us, hear our Christian teaching, and witness our Christian life. If some of them should prove stiff-necked, what of it? After all, we ourselves are not all good Christians either.[18]

Luther's own attempts to convert Jews proved unsuccessful. In 1526, when three rabbis visited him and discussed issues of biblical interpretation, Luther accused them of abusing texts and escaping from their true meaning; the encounter ended without mutual hatred.[19] However, rumors of Jewish plots and conspiracies against Luther aggravated the situation. Seemingly too busy to check these rumors out, Luther simply believed what he had heard and saw in them the confirmation of his conviction that Jewish hardened hearts were destined only to become harder. Some of Luther's friends and supporters advocated a return to such Jewish laws as the preservation of the Sabbath.

Such biblicism and narrow-mindedness finally got to Luther, and he denounced these "Sabbatarians" as "apes of the Jews" in 1535.[20] Convinced that Jews had organized a drive to convert Christians, Luther concluded that stern anti-Jewish measures were in order. So he supported Elector John Frederick's decree in 1536 which prohibited Jewish settlements in electoral Saxony. He also refused the request of Rabbi Josel of Rosheim to arrange for safe passage through Saxony. In a letter to Josel dated June 11, 1537 Luther declared that he was no longer willing to be manipulated into supporting Jewish presence in Germany.[21] He was also heard to say that he was done with "Jewish rascals" who "injure people in body and property," and that he'd write this Jew not to return to Saxony.[22] The good relations between Rabbi Josel and Luther had come to an end. The old established anti-Jewish ideology easily won Luther over, due in large measure to his frustration over the issue of Jewish conversion.

By 1537 Luther had concluded that the reconciliation between Israel and the Christian gospel was God's affair rather than the church's obligation. He could indeed have left the matter in God's hands—just as he did in matters of divine omnipresence and other mysteries of divine majesty and power—yet he felt compelled to offer his own interpretation of God's dealings with the Jews. In an open letter to his friend, Count Wolfgang

Schlick, who was the source of all the anti-Jewish rumors, Luther vented his frustration in 1538 by offering his own conclusion:

> Since fifteen hundred years of exile, of which there is no end in sight, nor can there be, do not humble the Jews or bring them to awareness, you may with good conscience despair of them. For it is impossible that God would leave his people without comfort and prophecy so long.[23]

It was not Luther's theological style to impose logical conclusions on God. Speculations about the "hidden" God, Luther usually contended, were out of order and led to the self-righteousness of a "theology of glory." "Things above us are no business of ours," he had told Erasmus in 1525 when Humanists speculated about the metaphysical implications of human freedom.[24] Some Luther scholars have argued that it was Luther's apocalyptic expectation of the end-time which inspired him to forego any and all attempts to evangelize the opposition—be they Jews, Papists, Turks or *Schwarmer* (opponents in his own camp "swarming" like bees about him). The Jews, more than any other group, disclosed to Luther the abominable self-righteousness which is the cancer for which God's wrath is the only cure.

The rest is sad history. Luther did not stop attacking the Jews, even after he had concluded that one must despair over the question of Christian–Jewish relations. He had drawn the same conclusion about the papacy, but continued to vent his angry frustration about it as "an institution of the devil."[25] So Luther spent his final years blasting away at the Jews. Perhaps Luther should have died before he wrote his vitriolic tracts against the Jews in the 1540s.[26] But Luther did not die, and he published the tracts which have branded him the spiritual ancestor of modern German anti-Semitism.

Luther did not change his mind from a friendly to a hostile attitude between the 1520s and 40s, as some interpreters have thought.[27] The issue for him was still the same: the christological interpretation of the Old Testament. Toward the end of his life, Luther pursued this question with intensity in his lectures on Genesis, and the so-called writings against the Jews must be seen within this context. Thus Luther's opposition to the Jews was not generic, in the sense that he hated whatever was Jewish. Rather, "the Jews *post Christum* represented for him the opposite of the believing Jews in the Bible."[28] Moreover, as odd as it may seem by hindsight, Luther wanted to preserve the religious, cultural, and political uniformity of a Christendom during the last days of the world before Christ's second coming. Consequently, he supported laws which prescribed the death penalty for those who denied the dogma of the Trinity, repeated

Christian baptism, as Anabaptists did, or rebelled against authority, as was the case with the Saxon peasants. They were all seditious and deserved to be severely punished by the ancient laws of Christendom. Luther could not conceive of a pluralistic society in which people would live together and still have differing faiths, or even belong to non-Christian traditions. To Luther the papists were heretical, the radicals in his own camp were blasphemous and seditious, the Turks were a foreign military threat, and the Jews were a fifth column within established Christendom. All of them had to be opposed in one way or another.

Towards the end of his life, Luther became convinced that Jews must be totally segregated from Christians, and this is the basic thrust of his infamous tract "On the Jews and Their Lies," 1543. After repeating the old arguments in favor of a christological interpretation of the Old Testament (the major portion of the tract), Luther followed through with a proposal for segregating the Jews. This proposal can be read as a prefiguration of the "final solution" proposed under Hitler: synagogues and Jewish schools are to be eliminated, if need be by burning; private Jewish Jewish schools are to be eliminated, if need be by burning; private Jewish homes are to be torn down in favor of communal, supervised settlements; Jewish literature is to be confiscated because it is blasphemous; Jewish migration is to be stopped; Jewish money is to be used for the support of converts; and Jews are to be put to work in order to stop their usury. "Gentle mercy will only tend to make them worse and worse," Luther advised, "while sharp mercy will reform them but little. Therefore, in any case, away with them!"[29] Many Christians and Jews expressed their deep shock over Luther's outbursts (among them Rabbi Josel of Rosheim, Luther's friend Philip Melanchthon, and the Nuremberg disciple Andreas Osiander), but he ignored them and, perhaps to spite them, published two more tracts, one "On the *Shem Hamphoras* [the name of the Lord exposed] and the Geneology of Christ" and the other on "The Last Words of David" (2 Sam. 23:1-7).[30] In all three tracts Luther disclosed how greatly he was influenced by the extremely successful anti-Jewish propaganda disseminated by Anthony Margaritha, who had deserted his prominent rabbinic family to convert to Christianity in 1522. Margaritha's popular work, *The Whole Jewish Faith* (*Der ganze judische Glaube*) presented a collection of the grossest anti-Christian polemics he claimed to be Jewish, most of which turned out to be false. The authorities of Augsburg finally expelled him after the Jewish community successfully proved that Margaritha was lying. Nevertheless, the deed was done and Margaritha was praised by the Christian establishment in Germany and elsewhere. Luther had swallowed these anti-Christian polemics hook, line, and sinker—and struck back with equally slanderous anti-Jewish polemics based on christological interpretations of the Old Testament. "I am done with the Jews," he concluded the tract on the *Shem Hamphoras*.[31] Yet almost immediately he began another tract on David! As a matter of fact, Luther could not extricate himself from what had become his "bete noire" (literally "black beast"). In his last sermon, preached on February 15, 1546 in his native town Eisleben three days before his death, he rambled about the end-time's satanic forces, especially the Jews. "If they turn from their blasphemies, we must gladly forgive them, but if not we must not suffer them to remain."[32] A pathetic epilogue indeed![33]

A Framework For Dialogue

Protestant, Catholic, and Jewish scholars have interpreted Luther's attitude to the Jews in various but often quite convergent ways.[34] Four major emphases can be clearly discerned in these interpretations:

1. There is a basic difference between the young and the old Luther. This interpretation, quite popular in regard to other aspects of Luther's life and thought, depicts Luther as a friend of the Jews until 1523, when he was accused by Catholic opponents as a "Judaizer." Until that time Luther expected a rapprochement between Christians and Jews, hoping for their conversion. But when he heard of Jewish attempts to convert Christians and saw Jewish influences in his own camp, such as the "Sabbatarians," he advocated a radical program of segregation, thus joining the defenders of the status quo in the sixteenth century.

2. Luther's anti-Jewish stance was fueled by a radical apocalyptic world view. This interpretation, strongly advanced most recently,[35] pictures a Luther who saw himself as one of the last voices in the wilderness of the end-time. To this extent, he was caught between God and Satan, with whose power Luther was constantly preoccupied. Luther rediscovered the radical gospel of God's unconditional promise of salvation through the righteousness of Jesus Christ, a righteousness which is to be appropriated by faith alone in Christ alone, without the benefit of reward for the works of love. This rediscovery of God's unconditional love in Christ was matched, so the interpretation goes, by a rediscovery of the biblical Satan who tempts believers to return to the power of self-righteousness through obedience to law, especially Jewish law. The Jews, therefore, were to Luther the principal embodiment of Satan's work at the end-time. They were to be completely avoided and segregated from Christians.

3. The so-called anti-Semitic writings of the old Luther were the product of sheer frustration over Christian failures to convert Jews, and Luther was too ill to be his true self. This interpretation, strongly leaning toward psychological norms, pictures Luther as the old priest-professor who had succumbed to gall stones, kidney stones, depressions, severe headaches, angina pectoris and other psychosomatic conditions which allowed Luther to fall victim to a rampant anti-Semitism. He was no longer capable, in contrast to healthier days, to make critical distinctions between fact and fiction when he read the charges levelled against Jews by fanatic Jewish converts. That is why Luther's final outbursts against Jews, as well as against the papacy, should be dismissed as the fulminations of a sick mind.

4. Luther's attitude never really changed. He stuck to the view, already clearly advanced in the first lectures on Psalms in 1513, that the Jews were the people of God who had received God's promise of an eternal relationship with him. This promise was fulfilled in Jesus Christ, the "second Adam," who died and was resurrected for the sake of sealing the given promise once and for all since the descendants of the "first Adam" had chosen to go their own way rather then the way of God. The restoration of the old relationship with God and redemption from the sin of self-righteousness depended totally on complete trust in Jesus Christ. Luther was convinced that such trust linked Jews and Christians, the Old and the New Testament, the Christian gospel and the history of Israel. When he, like others before him during the long history of Christianity, sensed failure to convert the Jews, he concluded that such was the will of God. Hence, Christians and Jews were to be totally separated, if need be by force.

It is this interpretation which suggests itself as the most plausible in the light of a critical reading of Luther's life and thought. But careful distinctions must be made between the sixteenth century and our own time before conclusions can be drawn as to the question whether or not Luther was an anti-Semite. Medieval and sixteenth-century Christian rejection of Jews was grounded in what can be called a theological anti-Judaism, rather than ethnic, indeed racist, anti-Semitism. The latter is the result of anthropological and sociological speculations associated with nonreligious attitudes toward nature and human nature. The cradle of such anti-Semitism is eighteenth-century Europe.[36] The history of this anti-Semitism is grounded in theories about an "Aryan race," a myth which is linked to varied speculations about human origins, ranging from Darwinism to continental European spiritualism.[37] The names of Comte Arthur de Gobineau (1816–82), John Houston Chamberlain, and Richard Wagner appear in the historical scenario of the origins of modern racism.

The term "anti-Semitism" itself may not have appeared before the 1870s, when the German Wilhelm Marr founded the first "League of Anti-Semitism" in 1879.[38] Thus it is not really appropriate to call Luther the father of modern, or even German, anti-Semitism.[39] Luther was very much the son of a medieval Christendom when he feared religious pluralism and advocated cruel means to preserve cultural uniformity, be it in his opposition to rebellious peasants or to Jews who were unwilling to convert to Christianity. But the thesis that Luther was "a child of his time" does not exonerate him from the charge that he was a sixteenth-century anti-Semite. He was. This should be flatly acknowledged.

The question is: why did Luther not develop the same critical attitude toward rampant anti-Semitism that he did toward the rampant deformation of the church which in turn caused a radical deformation of society? This is the critical issue emerging from Luther research. But any dialogue about this issue must also take into consideration a certain framework suggested by a critical reading of Luther and of history. Three essential aspects of this framework cannot be ignored:

1. Neither Luther's life nor his work were dominated by the issue of anti-Semitism. As priest, professor, and reformer Luther consistently wrestled with the Old Testament. But he did not single out Christian attitudes toward Jews as the principal issue. He was equally concerned with, and violent about, the papacy, the Anabaptists, and the rebellious peasants. They, as well as the Jews, had to be opposed, Luther contended, because they either identified their cause completely with the gospel of Jesus Christ, or rejected this gospel altogether on the basis of what Luther perceived to be a satanic, stubborn self-righteousness. To Luther the gospel was *the* issue in the sixteenth century—the cheering news that God's love for his people continued and was most clearly manifested in the man Jesus, thus linking Israel to Christendom as the one people of God who must live to proclaim the promise of God's unconditional covenant of love. Luther clearly communicated his basic stance in the significant tract, "Luther's Warning to His Dear German People" in 1531; he would risk war against pope and emperor if they rejected the promise of the gospel summarized in the statement that one is right with God by faith and trust alone rather than by "good works"—Paul's formulation in the Letter to the Romans (3:28)—for those who do not trust this gospel are worse than non-Christian Turks, heathen, or Jews. Christ must be glorified, even if the world goes to ruin over it. He, Luther, might die in the process, but . . . "Whatever evil they inflict on me, I will outdo them. No matter how hard their heads may be, they will find mine still harder. . . . I will survive, they will perish."[40]

2. Luther's "final solution" for the Jews must be seen in this context of urgent exhortation in the midst of a fast-moving reform movement which was threatened by various forces from within and without. Moreover, such final solutions had been proposed earlier by others. The highly respected German Catholic jurist and Humanist Ulrich Zasius had proposed quite similar measures against Jews in 1508. Luther may have been influenced by Zasius, who had expressed concerns shared by many lawyers and princes.[41] When it was Luther who spoke against the Jews, it seemed more significant, of course. But Zasius, Luther and others were agreed that, whatever needed to be done about whatever issue, it must be done in a legal and orderly way. Luther opposed any and all mob action, in contradistinction to other reformers like Baltahasar Hubmaier in Regensburg, who in 1519 told a mob to expel the Jews. Mob action and sedition were to Luther the most satanic ways of settling matters. Thus he called upon legitimate government, be it in church or state, when he demanded that measures be taken against the Jews. To modern ears this may sound irrelevant, but it was quite rare in the sixteenth century, rampant with violence and deliberate lawlessness.

To be sure, Luther shared anti-Semitic superstitions: synagogues must be burned because they were the home of the devil; Jews must be made to work the land because this was the most honest way to earn a living; and Christians must be protected from any Jewish influence because such influence would lead to sedition in a uniform Christian culture. Thus Luther did what any other leader in medieval Christendom either did or would have done. Southwestern Europe, for example, especially Spain and Portugal, had carried out such solutions and had initiated persecution of Jews.

Fortunately, hardly anyone heeded Luther's advice in 1543, although Jews were expelled from Saxony, as they had been expelled from other places in Europe. But no great effort was made to convert Luther's rhetoric into action. Nevertheless, Luther could have adhered to his earlier position to let "the spirits clash," as he put it—in this case, the Christian and Jewish spirits. Instead, Luther became as banal in his adaptation to the evil of anti-Semitism as everyone else was. The problem with evil, of course, is precisely that: it is so banal.[42]

3. Luther succumbed to the evil of anti-Semitism through a theological failure of nerve. He so desperately tried to communicate God's unconditional love for Israel as well as for the people of God called "Christians" that he could not stop moving from the proclamation of divine mercy to conclusions about God's wrath. Suddenly the usual proper distinctions, so brilliantly maintained with great theological sagacity in the midst of storm and stress, disappeared from Luther's vision. When faced with what he

considered self-righteous Jewish stubbornness in the matter of conversion, Luther no longer let God be God. Instead, he got all caught up in answers he himself so stubbornly had warned against. One *can* know the hidden God with regard to his plans for the Jews: God had rejected them and is in favor of their rejection in the world he created!

Even though Luther succumbed to judgments which made him a sixteenth-century anti-Semite, the movement which bears his name has never been committed just to him. He himself refused to accept the name "Lutheran" for his movement because he was, after all, only "poor stinking, maggot-fodder," as he put it with sincerity rather than false humility.[43] Lutherans should know better than most Christians that what makes and breaks the people of God is constant vigilance in obedience to the First Commandment of the Decalogue, "I am your God, you shall not have other gods." There is always the serpent's way, so well expressed in the story of the fall, which tempts us "to be like God" (Gen. 3:5). The issue for Christians and Jews alike is vigilance against idolatry—against the desire to dominate and to have control over others. No one is safe from this temptation, and everyone can become a fascist in the sense of either liking to be told what to do, or enjoying telling others what to do. History is full of such idolatrous incidents.

Those who honor Luther must honor the First Commandment and must, like Doberman Pinchers, guard against the abuse of human relationships, which are under God's mysterious rule. Luther's life and work was dedicated to "letting God be God"—the gracious God whose wrath remains hidden, though real. Nevertheless, he ended up trying to control a portion of the people of God, the Jews, whom he had called his own blood relatives. Thus Luther too violated the commandment to love thy neighbor in need, to be "a Christ to the neighbor," as he liked to put it. Tragically, his love for the Old Testament made him so jealous of the Jews—who claimed salvation without Jesus—that he turned into a harsh critic of Judaism and pronounced it the manifestation of God's wrath.

When Luther himself was in trouble with his own church and felt persecuted, especially in the 1520s, he felt a historical identity with Jews as the people of God without security in the world. There was a "third" or "radical Reformation"[44] (besides that of Luther and Calvin)—Mennonites, Anti-Trinitarians, Puritans and others—whose members became refugees in the face of sixteenth-century intolerance and were persecuted by the laws of sixteenth-century territorialism. They continued to experience what Luther felt, for a short time, in the early days of his reform movement. These religious refugees, who eventually could find a home only in the United States, are the bridge between an intolerant "magisterial

Reformation"[45] and a reformation which, as Luther envisaged it, was propelled by the mandate of the Christian gospel not to conform to this world. The time would come when these suffering reformers of the sixteenth century also succumbed to the enduring temptation "to be like God" when the pressure of persecution ceased. No one seems safe from a fall from faith to unfaith.

Luther's attitude to the Jews illustrates the fragility of faith in a world plagued by suffering, evil, and death. Despite pioneering insights into the universality of God's love, Luther turned the "good news" of this love into "bad news" for Jews and others whose hearts seemed to him so hardened that they could not become Christians. But given Luther's own view of Israel and the Old Testament, there really is no need for any Christian mission to the Jews. They are and remain the people of God, even if they do not accept Jesus Christ as their Messiah. Why this is so only God knows. Christians should concentrate their missionary activities on those who do not yet belong to the people of God, and they should court them with a wholistic witness in word and deed rather than with polemical argument and cultural legislation. Besides, the long history of Christian anti-Semitism calls for repentance rather than triumphalist claims of spiritual superiority.

Luther may not be of much help to post-Hitler Christians on the *via dolorosa* toward better Christian–Jewish relations. But as long as anti-Semitism survives among Christians, Luther cannot take the lion's share of the blame. We honor him best when we search our own hearts and cleanse our own minds from at least those evils which prevent us from living in tolerant solidarity with others.

REV. ERIC W. GRITSCH, Ph.D.
Professor of Church History
Director, Institute for Luther Studies
Lutheran Theological Seminary
Gettysburg, Pa.

Notes

1. This has been well documented in the comprehensive treatment of Salo W. Baron, *A Social and Political History of the Jews*, Vol. XIII: *Inquisition, Renaissance, and Reformation* (New York: Columbia University Press, 1969). See also Guido Kisch, *The Jews in Medieval Germany: A Study of Their Legal and Social Status* (Chicago: University

Notes

of Chicago Press, 1949). Quite informative is Léon Poliakov, *The History of Antisemitism*: *From the Time of Christ to the Court Jews* (Tr. Richard Howard; New York: Schocken Books, 1974), esp. ch. 10 on Luther and Germany.

2. See the original document in Heiko A. Oberman, *Die Wurzeln des Anti-Semitismus [The Roots of Anti-Semitism]* (Berlin: Severin and Siedler, 1982), Appendix, pp. 197-200.
3. *Ibid.*, ch. 10.
4. *Ibid.*, p. 50.
5. Quoted *ibid*, p. 50 from Erasmus' letter to Hochstraten, dated August 11, 1519.
6. Quoted in Oberman, p. 51 from Erasmus' letter to Capito, dated February 26, 1517.
7. Quoted in Oberman, p. 127 from the "Mandate Against the Jews" (*Mandat gegen die Juden*). The bishop was also Duke of Bavaria (1486–1529).
8. See Jerome Friedman, "The Reformation in Alien Eyes: Jewish Perceptions of Christian Troubles," *The Sixteenth Century Journal*, 14 (1983), 33. Friedman detects four Jewish approaches to the Reformation: doctrinal, historical, apocalyptic, and pragmatic-political (represented by Josel of Rosheim in Germany).
9. *Ibid.*, p. 34.
10. See, for example, Heinrich Bornkamm, *Luther and the Old Testament* (Tr. Eric W. and Ruth C. Gritsch; Philadelphia: Fortress), p. 7.
11. *Ibid.*, p. 250.
12. First Lectures on the Psalms, 1513–15. *Luther's Works* (American Edition, 55 vols.; Philadelphia: Fortress; St. Louis: Concordia, 1955–   ), 11, 17. Hereafter cited as LW.
13. *Ibid.* On Luther's use of medieval Old Testament exegesis, leading to the discovery of the "faithful synagogue" see James H. Preus, *From Shadow to Promise. Old Testament Interpretation From Augustine to Luther* (Cambridge, Mass.: Harvard University Press, 1974), ch. 14.
14. Lectures on Romans, 1515-16. LW 25, 182.
15. The Magnificat, 1521. LW 21, 354-55.
16. *In Refutation of a Jew-Book (Ains Judenbuechlins Verlegung)*, 1541. Quoted in Oberman, *op. cit.*, 47. Eck referred to Luther's love of the Hebrew language.
17. That Jesus Christ Was Born a Jew, 1523. LW 45, 200-01.
18. *Ibid.*, 229.
19. Sermon on Jerem. 23:5-9, November 25, 1526. *D. Martin Luthers Werke*. Kritische Gesamtausgabe (Weimar: Bohlau, 1833–   ), 20, 569:36-37. Hereafter cited as WA. Table Talk between May 21 and June 11, 1540. NO. 5026. WA Tischreden (Weimar: Bohlaus' Nachfolger, 1912–21), 4, 620:5-8. Hereafter cited as WA.TR.
20. Lectures on Genesis, 1535–36. LW 2, 361-62.
20. Lectures on Genesis, 1535-36. LW 2, 361-62.
21. WA Briefwechsel (Weimar: Bohlaus Nachfolger, 1930–48), 8, (89:9—90:13). Hereafter cited as WA.BR. On Josel of Rosheim see the comprehensive biography of Selma Stern, *Josel of Rosheim: Commander of Jewry in the Holy Roman Empire of the German Nation* (Tr. Gertrude Hirschler; Philadelphia: Jewish Publication Society, 1965).
22. Table Talk between May 27 and June 18, 1537. No. 3597. LW 54, 239.
23. Against the Sabbatarians, 1538. LW 47, 96.
24. The Bondage of the Will, 1525. LW 33, 139.
25. Against the Roman Papacy, and Institution of the Devil, 1545. LW 41, 259-376. This tract discloses the old Luther's radical language of violence.
26. See Roland H. Bainton, *Here I Stand: A Life of Martin Luther* (New York: Abingdon and Cokesbury, 1950), p. 379.

Notes

27. See, for example, Reinhold Lewin, *Luthers Stellung zu den Juden* (Berlin: Trowitzsch and Son, 1911). Rabbi Lewin's study is still unsurpassed in its nonideological research method and detailed analysis. Lewin influenced many other studies. The best summary of research is only available in German. See Johannes Brosseder, *Luthers Stellung zu den Juden im Spiegel seiner Interpretation* (Munchen: Hueber, 1972).

28. Aarne Siirala, "Luther and the Jews", *Lutheran World*, 11 (1964), 353.

29. On the Jews and Their Lies, 1543. LW 47, 272. See also pp. 268-72.

30. Not translated. *Vom Schem Hamphoras und vom Geschlecht Christi*, 1543. WA 53, 573-648. *Von den letzten Worten Davids*, 1543. WA 54, 16-100.

31. WA 53, 648: 11-12.

32. Warning to the Jews (*Eine Vermahnung an die Juden*), 1546. WA 51, 196:14-17. An appendix to the sermon.

33. See E. Gordon Rupp, "Martin Luther and the Jews", *Nederlands Theologisch Tijdschrift*, 31 (1977), 134.

34. Scholarship until 1972 is summarized and analyzed by Brosseder, *op. cit.* Latest literature cited in Mark U. Edwards, *Luther's Last Battles: Politics and Polemics* (Ithaca, N.Y.: Cornell University Press, 1983), ch. 6.

35. See Oberman, *op. cit.* In his recent Luther biography Oberman pictured Luther as "a man between God and Satan": *Luther. Mensch zwischen Gott und Satan* (Berlin: Severin and Siedler, 1982). To be published in English by Harvard University Press.

36. See George L. Mosse, *Toward the Final Solution: A History of European Racism* (New York: Howard Fertig, 1978), p. 1.

37. *Ibid.*, Part I.

38. How the history of anti-Semitism led to such a league and became significant for Hitler's ideology is well sketched in "Antisemitism," *Encyclopedia Judaica* (16 vols.; New York: Macmillan, 1971–72), 3, 87-160.

39. This became a popular notion in England after World War II. The British scholar E. Gorden Rupp disclosed how ridiculous this notion was in the face of historical data. See Peter C. Matheson, "Luther and Hitler: A Controversy Reviewed," *Journal of Ecumenical Studies* 17 (1980), 445-53.

40. Luther's Warning to His Dear German People, 1531. LW 47, 15-16.

41. See Guido Kisch, *Zasius und Reuchlein* (Pforzheimer Reuchlinschriften, 1; Konstanz and Stuttgart, 1961), p. 13.

42. See Hannah Ahrendt, *Eichmann in Jerusalem. A Report of the Banality of Evil* (New York: Viking, 1963).

43. A Sincere Admonition by Martin Luther to All Christians to Guard Against Insurrection and Rebellion, 1522. LW 45, 70-71.

44. Its history has been told by George H. Williams, *The Radical Reformation* (Philadelphia: Westminster, 1962). Oberman, *Die Wurzeln des Antisemitismus* calls the "third Reformation" the movement of Calvin who encouraged Protestantism in the cities. When the cities failed to be tolerant, religious refugees created an international movement which might help to provide some clues in improving the "stoney road to coexistence" between Christians and Jews. *Ibid.*, p. 187 and "Epilogue."

45. Williams' (*op. cit.*, p. xxiv) term for the Reformation which became aligned with princes and "magistrates."

10

The Reception of Luther's Writings on the Jews from the Reformation to the End of the 19th Century

Dr. Johannes Wallmann

This paper was prepared for a colloquium to explore the effect of Luther's anti-Semitic writings, cosponsored by the Division for Theological Studies of the Lutheran Council in the USA and the American Jewish Committee, October 11–13, 1983. Dr. Wallmann makes it clear that Luther's writings were not the source of anti-Semitism during the 400 years between the Reformation and the rise of the Nazis. There were Lutherans and others who believed and publicized anti-Semitic ideas, but Luther was not their source, and the ideas are not inherent in Lutheranism.

Much has been written about Martin Luther's attitude toward the Jews. But we know very little about the effects which were brought about by Luther's writings on the Jews: Alex Bein writes in his scholarly work "The Jewish Question. Biography of a World Problem": "This is not the place to document in detail the influence which Luther's anti-Jewish opinions and writings exercised on his contemporaries and subsequent generations— and moreover sufficient scholarly research is lacking in this area."[1] In the annotations to his work, Bein again expresses this opinion: "There has not been, as far as I know, a scholarly study of the influence of Luther's portrayal of the Jews which considers all aspects of the question."[2]

I am quoting this thorough and exacting Israeli historian at this early point in order to demonstrate that my talk represents a somewhat risky undertaking. I shall be entering upon a kind of no-man's-land of historical research. Initial investigations exist only for the 2nd half of the 19th and for the 20th century. We have for this period the work of Johannes Brosseder: "Luther's Attitude toward the Jews as Reflected by his Interpretors. The Interpretation and Reception of Luther's Writings and Remarks on Judaism in the 19th and 20th Centuries, Principally in German-speaking Countries."[3] For the period from the Reformation to the early 19th century no research at all has been done. Anyone doing pioneer work in this no-man's-land of research must rely on a forbearing audience and can hardly hope to produce with an initial attempt a study which "considers all aspects of the question," as Bein demands. But by examining the sources, he will perhaps be able to cast some light into an area which is at present covered by darkness. It is indeed a darkness of such intensity that it has made possible the existence of two completely opposed and mutually exclusive assertions: on the one hand the contention that Luther's anti-Jewish writings and opinions exercised a major and persistent influence in the centuries after the Reformation and that he was one of the fathers of modern anti-Semitism. A direct historical line of influence is thus established from Luther to modern anti-Semitism up to Hitler. On the other hand there is the assertion that Luther's anti-Jewish writings have had no influence at all, that in Germany the pro-Jewish attitude of the young reformer of 1523 rather than the anti-Jewish standpoint of the aged Luther has prevailed. According to this opinion there is no historical continuity between Luther and modern anti-Semitism, which, however, says nothing about the question whether this lack of continuity is to be evaluated in a positive sense or, as in the case of the racial ideologists of the "Third Reich," in a negative one.

The assertion that Luther's expressions of anti-Jewish sentiment have been of major and persistent influence in the centuries after the Reformation, and that there exists a continuity between Protestant anti-Judaism and modern racially oriented anti-Semitism is at present widespread in the literature; since the Second World War it has understandably become the prevailing opinion. It would be superfluous to present documentary evidence to this effect. Even in cases where it is recognized that Luther had no sucess with his suggestion to burn the synagogues and expel the Jews, still it is assumed that his anti-Jewish attitude exercised a formative influence on Protestantism. Franz Heinrich Philipp, for example, wrote in the periodical "Emuna" in 1972: "It is true that Luther's suggestions concerning the treatment of the Jews were ignored or expressly rejected by the Protestant princes. Yet his attitude in the Jewish question continued to be the decisive factor in determining the standpoint of the Lutheran Church in the succeeding centuries, and a one-sided selection of his opinions formed a standard part of polemic anti-Semitic literature well into the 20th century."[4] We have here the classic expression of what I call the *continuity thesis*: the assertion that, starting with the anti-Judaical writings of the aged Luther, the attitude of the Lutheran Church has been essentially and continually inimical to the Jews, and that for this reason Lutheranism has been especially susceptible to the poison of modern racially oriented anti-Semitism.

The opposing contention is nowadays less frequent: namely, that Luther's late anti-Jewish writings have had no lasting influence in the centuries succeeding the Reformation, and that there is no historical continuity between Luther's religious anti-Judaism and modern anti-Semitism. This was the prevailing opinion during the period before 1933, and it was thus the opinion generally accepted by the racial ideologists of the Third Reich. Practically all the writers of Hitler's time who, by making references to Luther's opinions about the Jews, attempted to legitimize the national socialist enmity against them voiced the complaint that Luther's struggle against the Jews was unknown, that it had been concealed by the Lutheran Church for centuries, and that Luther's writings on the Jews had completely fallen into obscurity. The anti-Semitic propaganda sheet "Der Sturmer" lamented in November, 1933, that not one of the numerous publications which appeared in commemoration of Luther's 450th birthday mentioned his struggle against the Jews. "It seems apparent that even now this struggle is meant to be concealed."[5] Walther Linden, who published "Luther's Treatises against the Jews" in 1935, woefully maintained that Luther's work with the title "On the Jews and their Lies" had been unknown throughout the period from the Reformation to the 20th century. He writes: "To no considerable extent has this work of Luther's attained success up to our own day. This work of majestic linguistic power, written for the people, has not reached the people at all. The Jewish propagandists, most significantly Josel von Rosheim, have done everything to prevent its becoming known."[6] The following passage occurs as late as 1940 in the foreword to an annotated edition of Luther "On the Jews and their Lies" and "On *Schem Hamphoras*": "It is characteristic enough of the Power of the Jews and of the ineradicable pro-Jewish attitude of the theologians, that both of these works—so significant in evaluating the Jewish question—have until now remained practically unknown. They are not included at all in most of the complete editions of Luther's works."[7]

This latter statement—that Luther's writings about the Jews had not been included in most of the complete editions—was absurd: the fact is that they were published in all of the complete editions beginning with the

Wittenberg and Jena edition of the 16th century and including the Weimar edition of the 20th century. This of course is no indication of how well-known they were, or of their reception and influence. The comprehensive editions of Luther's works—the Weimar edition consists of more than 100 volumes in lexicon format—have from the beginning been consulted by only a few users, almost exclusively by scholars. It is the selected editions of his works which have been the decisive factor in the reception of Luther: these editions have been the source of knowledge about him for the average theologian and for educated laymen. And it is in fact true that none of the selected editions of the 19th and the early 20th century contain the writings about the Jews. The inefficacy of Luther's anti-Jewish writings will have to remain a debatable thesis until the contrary can be proved. It is in any case an opinion which is maintained by serious scholars, both Christian and Jewish. Haim Hillel Ben Sasson, for example, in "A History of the Jewish People," states that Luther's writings against the Jews remained ineffectual because of historical circumstances, and that "it was rather the Luther of 1523 than the Luther of 1543 who remained predominant in the view of large segments of the Protestant world until well into the 20th century."[8]

We have thus two opposed answers to the question presented in our topic: on the one hand the thesis that Luther's anti-Jewish attitude exercised a major and continual influence on the period between the Reformation and the 20th century; on the other hand the thesis that Luther's influence in this regard was slight or nonexistent. I shall now attempt to give an answer of my own to this question.

In the last chapter of his book "Luther's Position with regard to the Jews," Reinhold Lewin has taken up the question of the influence of Luther's late work entitled "On the Jews and their Lies."[9] His answer is: The work had no appreciable influence among Luther's contemporaries. For in the first place it failed completely to attain the spectacular literary success which Luther's early work "That Jesus Christ Was Born a Jew" had enjoyed. This work, which was published in 1523, was reissued and reprinted a number of times and at various places; it became widely known, and was well received even in some cases by Jews themselves. There were two translations into Latin, which made it possible for the work to attain recognition even outside of German-speaking countries. "On the Jews and their Lies," however, was published in only two Wittenberg editions, and was not reprinted elsewhere. Josel von Rosheim was able to prevent its being reprinted in Strasburg. Only the Latin translation by Justus Jonas was relatively widely distributed, but in France and Italy instead of Germany.

This lack of literary success went hand in hand with the corresponding political failure of the work. Luther achieved success with this work only in the Electorate of Saxony. Here he was able to re-activate a decree expelling the Jews which had been issued in 1536 but relaxed in 1539. However, the Protestant princes and magistrates did not act upon Luther's suggestions. "The danger which he [Luther] evokes is by no means so great as the contemporary Jews initially fear, who consider themselves threatened in their very existence."[10]

Lewin's thesis concerning the inefficacy of Luther's late works on the Jews can be supported by still other data. At the time when Luther was openly attacking the Jews, the fundamental creed and doctrine of the Lutheran Church had already been established. Luther's rejection of his earlier pro-Jewish attitude, coming to the surface for the first time in 1537 in the letter to Rabbi Josel of Rosheim,[11] developed too late to have any influence on the formation of the Lutheran creed, which occurred between 1529 and 1536.[12] The significance of this for Lutheran doctrine can be made clear in a comparison with Luther's position as regards Islam.

During the early period of the Reformation, Luther's Catholic enemics, who were loyal to the Pope, considered him a friend of Jews as well as of Turks, that is of Islam.[13] It is in fact true that there are not only pro-Jewish opinions, but also laudatory remarks about Islam in his early reform works.[14] Just as in the case of Judaism, it seems that one could distinguish between an early pro-Islam and a later anti-Islam period. Yet as early as 1529, when the Turks were marching toward Vienna, Luther made it unmistakeably clear in his so-called "Turkish Works" that the Moslems were to be considered enemies of the Protestants.[15] The rejection of Islam is incorporated into the Lutheran confessions, for example the Confessio Augustana of 1530.[16] Mohammed is looked upon, after the pope, as the second great enemy of Christendom.[17] There is, in contrast, no rejection of Judaism in the writings on Lutheran doctrine and, apart from a remark in the apocryphal Latin version of "Formula of Concord," 1577,[18] there are no negative characterizations of contemporary Jews.

Lutheran ministers were for centuries bound to conform to Lutheran confessional writings which provided the guidelines on which they based their teachings. It was therefore of great significance that in these fundamental doctrines of their church the Islam was portrayed as enemy, but not the Jews. The result can be seen in the hymns and in the devotional literature of early Lutheranism; many Lutheran hymns are directed against Islam. Consider, for example, the original version of a famous hymn by Luther, still to be found in all Lutheran hymnbooks, "Lord, keep us steadfast in your word. Curb the murder by Pope and Turk."[19] Comparable hymns about the Jews are not known. There are in the Lutheran Church of the 16th century, as far as I know, no hymns about Christ's passion which, like Catholic hymns of the Middle Ages and later, refer to the Jews in connection with Christ's sufferings and give them the name "Murderers of Christ." Also in the classic devotional literature which appeared during early Lutheranism, such as Christian Scriver's "Treasure of the Soul," there is the definite portrayal of the Moslems as enemies, but no such portrayal of the Jews.[20] The medieval accusations made against the Jews of ritual murder and sacrileges committed against the Sacred Host are not repeated in the early Lutheran devotional literature.

For the decades after Luther's death all the evidence seems to support Lewin's thesis that Luther's late works on the Jews failed to achieve their intended effect. But a quarter of a century after Luther's death, the situation changes. Two works now appear which take it upon themselves to revive the struggle of the aged Luther against Judaism. The author of one of these works, which appeared in 1570, is Georg Nigrinus, pastor in Gieben. The title is "Enemy Jew."[21] The editor of the other work is the Leipzig professor of theology Nikolaus Selnecker, who was also a coauthor of the last of the Lutheran doctrinal works, the Formula of Concord. Selnecker published in 1577 an anthology of Luther's works on the Jews.[22] The volume includes "On the Jews and their Lies," "On *Schem Hamphoras,*" and in addition "Against the Sabbatarians." In these two books by Nigrinus and Selnecker we find for the first time the two literary forms in which Luther's anti-Judaism was to be handed down and made relevant for later periods: quotations of his "Suggestions" to the authorities for the treatment of Jews in connection with a plan for solving the Jewish problem (in Nigrinus' work), and the reprinting of his anti-Jewish writings in order to make them available again to the public (in the work of Selnecker). The reasons Selnecker gives for republishing the works are interesting: he writes that Luther's works against the Jews have up to now been suppressed, and that it is now necessary to make them available to the people again.

I will not be able here to give an account of the contents of these two works. A common element is the warning against the Jews as blasphemers and enemies of Christendom. They are, by the way, in this connection also characterized as secret allies of the Turks. The works are directed to different audiences. Nigrinus addresses himself to the authorities, in particular the Landgraves of Hessen, in order to enlighten them about the threat posed by the Jews. The authorities would do well, he says, to banish the Jews from their states. If the law now in force should make this impossible, then one should at least oppress them and follow Luther's suggestions for the treatment of the Jews. Luther had said: If harsh measures are not effective, the Jews should be driven out. Nigrinus says: If for legal reasons they cannot be driven out, they should at least be harshly suppressed. Nigrinus thus makes a stronger plea than Luther: he is in favor of banishing the Jews.

Instead of addressing himself to the authorities, as Nigrinus does, Selnecker directs his appeal to the businessmen in the large commercial cities and marketing centers. His intention is to keep them from having any intercourse with the Jews: he pleads with them not to engage in any form of contact with these blasphemers. While Nigrinus confines himself to the "Enemy Jew" alone, Selnecker includes the Jews among a group of enemies of the true Lutheran faith who had been anathematized in the same year by the Formula of Concord. "Sacramentalists, Calvinists, Enthusiasts, Jews and Epicureans are beside us and among us! God protect us!" Selnecker cries.[23] Apparently he was not satisfied that the Formula of Concord had anathematized the Sacramentalists, the Calvinists, the Enthusiasts, and the ungodly Epicureans, but had maintained silence about the Jews. The designation of the Jews as "obstinati et perditissimi homines" in the apocryphal Latin translation of the Formula of Concord[24] can probably be traced to Selnecker. His edition of Luther's writings on the Jews seems to be a kind of private supplement to the Formula of Concord.

The reception of Luther's late works on the Jews begins therefore only with Georg Nigrinus and Nikolaus Selnecker. In the decades before the Thirty Years' War two further separate editions of Luther's anti-Jewish treatises occur in imitation of Selnecker. "On the Jews and their Lies" is said to have been published in Dortmund in 1595, but confiscated by the Emperor under pressure from the Jews.[25] In Frankfurt am Main the three late anti-Jewish Treatises of Luther were published in 1613 and 1617.[26] It is striking that the publication of these works took place coincidentally with the banishing of the Jews from Frankfurt and Worms, the single large-scale expulsion of Jews from Lutheran cities in Germany known to have occurred before the 20th century.[27]

These three reprints dating from the decades before the Thirty Years' War remain the last popular editions of Luther's works on the Jews for hundreds of years, up until the 20th century. Luther's "Suggestions" for the treatment of Jews, however, continue to be handed down for quite some time in the "adverse Judaeos" literature, which was initiated with Georg Nigrinus' "Enemy Jew." The polemic literature against Judaism in the early days of the Lutheran Church is quite extensive and a comprehensive bibliography does not exist even today.[28] A prominent role in the production of this polemic literature was played by a number of Christianized Jews who, as successors of Johannes Pfefferkorn, took it upon themselves to attack their former fellow Jews, and to inform the Christians about Jewish teachings, rituals, and customs. Antonius Margaritha's "The Entirety of Jewish Belief," one of the major sources for Luther's late anti-Jewish works,[29] was republished in Frankfurt, 1544, 1561, 1686, and Leipzig, 1705.[30] In addition there were other baptized Jews, such as Ernst Ferdinand Hess, Samuel Friedrich Brentz, Christian Gerson, and others. The titles of some of their works demonstrate with what eagerness these writers continued the tradition of Pfefferkorn: "Scourge of the Jews,"[31] "Mirror of the Jews,"[32] "Cast-off Jewish Snakeskin."[33] Only one of these writers, Christian Gerson, makes reference to Luther's work of 1523.[34] All the others follow Nigrinus and warn against tolerating the Jews. All such anti-Jewish writings from the pens of Christianized Jews form the source material for a subsequent work which absorbs the information contained in them and, with its publication at the beginning of the 18th century becomes the standard anti-Jewish work and a kind of literary munitions arsenal for all later writers against the Jews: Andreas Eisenmenger, "Judaism Unmasked" (1711).[35]

It is well known that Eisenmenger functioned as a major source of evidence for the anti-Semites of the 19th and 20th centuries. His huge 2,000 page work, which was published again in abbreviated form in the late 19th century,[37] provided the anti-Semites up to Julius Streicher with a seemingly inexhaustible amount of material. What we are interested in here is the question: What was Eisenmenger's relationship to Luther?

It would hardly be possible to call him a second Luther. First of all: Eisenmenger's origins are in German Calvinism. He was not a Lutheran. The denominational barriers between Lutheranism and Calvinism were more pronounced in the 17th century than at any other time. Eisenmenger's father was an official in the service of the Calvinist Elector of the Palatinate. After completing his studies at the reformed University of Heidelberg, he was sent to continue his education in Holland and England.[38] Secondly: In the voluminous "Judaism Unmasked" an abundance of authorities are cited, for the most part Jewish or former Jewish authors, in smaller numbers Protestant specialists on Judaism who came, however, in general from the reformed areas of Switzerland and the Netherlands.[39] The name Luther does not appear in Eisenmenger's work. He is familiar with the "Enemy Jew" by Nigrinus, and once mentions Selnecker's edition of Luther's treatises, but only in order to refute a remark contained therein.[40] It is unlikely that he ever had firsthand contact with Luther's works. A third point: while anti-Jewish works make up only a small fraction of Luther's total literary productions, Eisenmenger spent his entire life studying and writing nothing but works on the Jews. For 19 years, from 1680 to 1699, he obsessively searched through Jewish literature. Eisenmenger's "Judaism Unmasked" is the work of a monomaniacal anti-Jew.

Theologically, as well, it is difficult to make any connection between Luther and Eisenmenger. Luther fought a battle for truth against falsehood. He was concerned with the truth contained in the Scriptures, above all, with the interpretation of the prophecies of the coming of Christ. Although Luther himself refused any further discussions with the Jews, disputations and discussions occurred repeatedly between Lutheran theologians and Jews, in the early 17th century in Wittenberg University, for example.[41] Eisenmenger is not concerned with the question of truth in the Scriptures. His intention is to "unmask," to expose what he considers to be the true face of Judaism. His source is not the Bible, but the Talmud, through the use of which he hopes to reveal the allegedly pernicious views and practices of the Jews. Eisenmenger put an end to the dialogue between Christians and Jews. In the process he repressed Luther rather than carry on his tradition. His "Judaism Unmasked" cast Luther's anti-Jewish writings into obscurity. Hardly any attention is in fact paid to them by the 18th and 19th century authors who write against Judaism and regularly make reference to Eisenmenger.

Before leaving Eisenmenger and continuing into the 18th and 19th centuries, we must take another brief look at the early 17th century. The authority of Luther was very important in deciding whether to tolerate the Jews in the individual German territories and cities. The question "an tolerandi in republica Christiana Judaei?" is frequently taken up by theologians of the 17th century, partly in opinions delivered at the behest of the authorities, partly in academic disputations, partly in theological textbooks under the heading "law and government."

Nigrinus and Selnecker, supported by the authority of Luther, had taken the position of Lutheran intolerance. They held the opinion that, as blasphemers, Jews should not be tolerated in Christian states. This position is adopted by other Lutheran theologians at the end of the 16th century, for example by Lukas Osiander in Tübingen, who protests against the acceptance of Jews and is for this reason removed from his official position by the Duke of Württemberg.[42] In a document preserved only in handwritten form, the famous Lutheran theologian Martin Chemnitz as well protested to the Duke of Braunschweig against the admission of Jews. Chemnitz makes express reference to Luther, and includes long quotations from his works on the Jews.[43] At the end of the 16th century Luther serves as an authority for intolerance toward the Jews.

In the early 17th century the picture surprisingly changes. In the year 1611 the Lutheran city of Hamburg asks theological experts in the faculties of Jena and Frankfurt an der Oder to deliver opinions whether the right to stay in the city could be granted to those Jews who had fled from Portugal. Both Lutheran faculties answer in the affirmative.[44] The theologians in Jena and Frankfurt an der Oder speak in favor of a toleration of the Jews, though only under certain conditions: prohibition of public worship (no synagogues) and restriction of civic rights. For the history of the German Jews it was of considerable importance that in addition to Amsterdam this large German commercial center as well, which had opposed the immigration of the Jews for centuries, opened its gates to them at the beginning of the 17th century.

In the opinion delivered by the Jena Theological Faculty in 1611 "Whether and how one should integrate and tolerate the Jews in Christian states" the authority of Martin Luther, in addition to a series of passages from the Bible, plays a decisive role. The Jena theologians referred to Luther's treatise of 1523 "That Jesus Christ Was Born a Jew" and quoted long passages from it.[45] They admitted that of course they were aware of the fact that elsewhere Luther considered the expulsion of the Jews, but to their mind Luther was in this case only thinking of it as a preventive measure against possible Jewish blasphemies.

The Jena theologians try to bring Luther's intolerant comments into line with his tolerant ones. The thought that Luther may have changed his attitude is as far from their minds as the idea that he may be contradicting himself. Therefore they lay down the hermeneutic rule that Luther's sharp words are to be interpreted against the background of his clear and friendly words in the treatise of 1523. The Luther of 1523 here becomes an authority "that in Christian states and towns Jews can well be tolerated and permitted."[46]

The command to be tolerant towards the Jews, which had been given by two Lutheran faculties, roused a lively discussion in Lutheranism. Never before nor since have so many papers on the question of tolerance as regards Jews been published as was the case after 1611. The result of this discussion is summarized by Johann Gerhard, the most important Lutheran theologian of the 17th century, in his major work "Loci theologici."[47] To begin with he says that the question "an tolerandi in republica Judaei" is negated by some theologians, and among them Luther. Luther is here no longer regarded as an authority in favor of tolerance. Basically, however, Gerhard keeps to the yes of the Jena faculty in the question of tolerance as regards Jews. But the conditions and restrictions which are to be imposed on the Jews are now formulated more sharply. Gerhard demands that they should be compelled to attend the Christian service, which had not been regarded as necessary in the opinion of the Jena faculty; furthermore he insists on the withdrawal of the Hebrew books and a clear social degradation. Luther's advice from the treatise "On the Jews and Their Lies," which had been ignored in the Jena opinion, is explicitly quoted, even if its realization in detail is not demanded. Instead of the Luther of 1523, who served as an example in the opinion delivered by the Jena faculty, the Luther of 1543 becomes predominant again. Most of the Lutheran theologians of the 17th century remain on Johann Gerhard's course, as, for example, Pastor Johannes Muller of Hamburg in his well-known book of 1644, "Judaism or the Jewish People."[48] With Johannes Muller the aged Luther from the treatises of 1543 is again copiously quoted. His advice as regards the treatment of Jews is cited and is also adopted, though with a number of moderations.[49] It is now interpreted as "conditions and suggestions according to which the Jews shall be tolerated among the Christians."[50]

The Lutheranism of the 17th century, as represented by its leading theologians, therefore, does know a "tolerantia limitata," as regards the Jews. It is not correct to say that only the representatives of jurisprudence in Germany advocated a "tolerantia limitata," but that the theologians on the other hand negated any tolerance whatsoever: in any case this does not apply to Lutheran areas. (This opinion was recently expressed by Wilhelm Gude, a disciple of Guido Kisch, in a paper entitled "The legal position of the Jews in the writings of German jurists of the 16th and 17th centuries"[51]). Whoever has read the memoirs of the Jewish merchant's wife (Gluckel of Hameln), this unique document of Jewish life from the 17th century, knows about the surprising possibilities of Jewish family and community life that existed within the bounds of this "tolerantia limitata."[52]

I have spoken in detail about the Lutheranism of the 17th century. With Pietism, that great pious movement of German Protestantism which developed at the end of the 17th century and which thoroughly reformed the character of the Lutheran Church, I can be briefer. It is well known that Pietism, on the basis of its chiliastic hopes for the future, criticized Luther's attitude as regards the Jews, especially where the question of the conversion of the Jews was concerned. This hope for a final conversion of the Jews, as expressed by St. Paul in his letter to the Romans (chapter 11:25 f.), is one of the central theological concerns of Pietism. It is also a well-known fact that pietistic writers frequently made reference to the young Luther. The anti-Jewish works Luther wrote later pose a problem for the Pietists. Philipp Jakob Spener, the founder of Pietism, was an authority on Luther's writings, and one of the few Lutheran theologians who had read Luther's complete works.[53] He knew Luther's anti-Jewish writings, but he never referred to these. Spener ignored them. When he comes to speak of the Jews in his sermons or papers, he is fond of quoting passages from Luther, but only pro-Jewish ones. For example, he talks in a sermon he preached in Frankfurt am Main in 1682 about the virtues of the Jewish people as the most noble of all races (Geschlechter) and here quotes Luther in support: "And just as our dear Luther thought it right that we should love all Jews for the sake of the one Jew Jesus, in the same way we are to hold their whole race in high esteem for the sake of this most noble of the Jews: Jesus."[54] Similarly Nikolaus Ludwig Count of Zinzendorf, the most important Pietist of the 18th century, quotes Luther when he gives the reasons why Christians should have a profound respect for the Jews: "Jesus was a Jew, and for that reason one should love all Jews, as Luther writes to the Jew, Josel von Rosheim."[55] In Pietism only the young pro-Jewish Luther is read. The radical Pietist Gottfried Arnold, author of the famous "History of the Church and of Heretics," gives detailed quotations from Luther's treatise "That Jesus Christ Was Born a Jew," and regards this as exemplary advice given by Luther to his followers. That Luther in later years revoked his positive advice of 1523 is openly criticized.[56] Johann Georg Walch, editor of the great Walch Luther edition and closely connected to Pietism, also does not refrain from overt criticism. He says that with his advice to burn the synagogues and deprive the Jews of their books, Luther, in his zeal, "did not keep within fair bounds, and went too far in this matter."[57]

The benevolent position of the Pietists with regard to the Jews and their corresponding distance to the opinions of the aged Luther called forth the opposition of the theologians of late Lutheran orthodoxy. This lead for a short time to an identification of the orthodox Lutheran theologians with the aged Luther, and to an intensification of the hostile attitude against Jews to a degree which cannot be found in the classical period of Lutheran orthodoxy in the 17th century. The most outrageous words of hatred against Jews which have ever been written by Lutheran theologians date from the early 18th century, the century of the Enlightenment. The Hamburg Pastor, Erdmann Neumeister, in his hatred and hostility against the Jews by far surpasses his predecessor Johannes Müller, who is notorious in the literature as a fierce hater of Jews. All medieval accusations up to and including the charge of ritual murder of Christian children are reiterated by Erdmann Neumeister.[58] His hostile portrayal of the Jews clearly influenced the article "Jews" in Zedler's *Grosses Universallexikon* (Comprehensive Encyclopedia)[59] and became thus presumably of great influence on the idea that the bourgeois classes in 18th-century Germany had of the Jews. Luther is neither mentioned nor quoted; Eisenmenger, however, is.[60]

The German Enlightenment, and in particular Lutheran theology during this period, was strongly influenced by the pietistic reform movement. This explains its attitude as regards the Jews, which is in general positive. Siegmund Jakob Baumgarten and Johann Salomo Semler, both theologians of Germany's largest theological faculty, in Halle an der Saale, and the two most important German theologians of the Enlightenment, do not show any traces of a hostile attitude as regards the Jews. Both of them even spoke very clearly against anti-Jewish tendencies. Siegmund Jakob Baumgarten made the strongest plea in this regard in a "theological opinion on the conscientious toleration of the Jews and their worship among the Christians which was written in 1745 at the request of some Jews.[61] Baumgarten's opinion is the most impressive evidence for the fact that the friendly attitude of Protestants as regards the Jews was not confined to the small circles of so-called philosemites. Baumgarten concedes without any restriction that the Jews have the right to their public worship. He even enjoins the Christians, especially the Protestants, who had themselves been the objects of persecution for religious reasons, "to actively express their disgust for the acts of violence against the Jews which had been committed by Christians to their gross dishonour."[62] Johann Salomo Semler in his statements pertaining to Reimarus' Wolfenbuttel fragments, published by Lessing, reacts sharply to Reimarus' scorning of the Jews:

"This scorning of the Jews . . . is truly inappropriate for a dignified humanitarian."[63] Semler is not sparing in his criticism about how the Jews in the past centuries had to suffer under the Christians: "Unfortunately the Christians have always inflicted great trouble, misery and oppression on this nation, to whom they owe so much. . . . For many centuries papal and imperial orders were needed to somewhat impede and restrain the foolish inhuman zeal, the spirit, the oppression and cruel persecution by the Christians. The Jews were much better off under the Romans, Greeks, and Moslems than was usually the case under the Christians."[64]

Thus among the most important Lutheran theologians of the Enlightenment no traces of the anti-Jewish attitude of the aged Luther can be found. Since Baumgarten and Semler derived from Pietism, it is tempting to place them in that tradition which began with Luther's pro-Jewish work of 1523. But Baumgarten and Semler, when they talk about Jews, never refer to Luther's writings on the Jews. In Baumgarten's great "History of the Religious Parties" one finds a detailed description of Judaism. A wealth of bibliographical references are given for the benefit of those who are concerned with the Jews: beginning with the writings of the Fathers of the Church, via Calvin, up to the orientalists of the 17th and 18th century. But Luther's writings on the Jews are not mentioned at all.[65] Thus we are confronted with a problem which makes it very difficult to carry out our task of investigating the influence of Luther on the modern attitude towards the Jews. From the early 18th century almost all traces of a further influence of Luther in this area disappeared. Whoever writes about Jews no longer mentions Luther's writings on them. Did Lessing, the friend of Mendelssohn and the author of "Nathan," have any knowledge at all of Luther's works on the Jews? I have asked friends, who know Lessing more thoroughly, about this matter, but there was no one who could answer this question. Obviously there is no evidence that he did. Did the philosophers of German Idealism, did Kant, Fichte, Hegel and Schelling have any knowledge of Luther's writings on the Jews? As far as I can see, this cannot be assumed. When Fichte in 1793 yielded to the temptation to express harsh anti-Jewish sentiments, Saul Ascher answers with a paper "Eisenmenger the second."[66] Eisenmenger was known as an enemy of the Jews, whereas Luther was not any longer. None of the great figures at the time of the German classical period had such a profound knowledge of Luther's writings as Johann Georg Hamann. Through his study of Luther Hamann gained a profound understanding of the Bible and of the special character of the Jewish religion; therefore he was able to criticise Moses Mendelssohn's attempt at a reconciliation of the Jewish religion with religion based on enlightened reason.[67] There is no indication that Hamann was familiar with Luther's works on the Jews. When he heard that Kant had given a contemptuous opinion on Lessing's "Nathan," he complained to Herder that Kant was not willing to accept a hero of Jewish origin.[68]

When we now pass on to the 19th century, at first nothing changes the impression, that Luther's writings on the Jews have fallen into oblivion. For the anti-Jewish wave at the beginning of the 19th century Eisenmenger is the great authority, for example in the case of Carl Wilhelm Grattenauer's "Against the Jews: A word of warning to all our Christian fellow citizens."[69] Grattenauer gives a rich bibliography of anti-Jewish writings—no mention of Luther. The philosopher Jakob Friedrich Fries, who in 1816 wrote "On the danger that arises to the prosperity and character of the German nation through the Jews" never refers to Luther.[70] Fries had, as a Jena professor, participated in the Wartburg Festival of the German students in 1817, where for the first time Jewish books had been thrown into the fire, accompanied by the shout: "Woe to the Jews." Neither Fries and the student participants nor Saul Ascher, a Jewish critic of the Wartburgfeier, probably knew anything of Luther's anti-Jewish writings.[71] Ernst Moritz Arndt, one of the spiritual fathers of writings.[71] Ernst Moritz Arndt, one of the spiritual fathers of popular German nationalism and furthermore a declared opponent of the Jews, is one of the few who had pursued thorough studies of Luther's writings. Among his posthumous papers we still have his notes on studies in the Walch Luther edition: From volume 14 and 15 Arndt goes straight on to volume 22 and 21, later to volume 19 and 18, leaving out volume 20 which contains Luther's writings on the Turks and the Jews.[72] In his youth the historian Leopold von Ranke read Luther's works extensively, as we have known since the publication of his so-called Luther fragments in 1817.[73] In his classic and frequently reprinted Work "German History in the age of the Reformation"(1839–1847) Ranke deals with the persecution of the Jews at the beginning of the 16th century and with the Reuchlin dispute. Not a word is said about Luther's attitude as regards the Jews.

At the present state of research it is not possible to say when for the first time in the 19th century attention is again drawn to Luther's works on the Jews.[74] There is cause to believe that the ban of oblivion was not lifted before the reprinting of Luther's late treatises on the Jews in the Erlangen Luther edition. The 32nd volume, which contained the late writings on the Jews, was published in 1832.[75] Only a couple of years later a paper appeared which, according to Reinhold Lewin, is the first in the 19th century to deal with the topic "Luther and the Jews": Ludwig Fischer, "Dr. Martin Luther. On the Jews and Their Lies. A condensed excerpt of his writings on the delusion of the Jews, their woe, conversion and future."[76] At intervals of several years further papers on that topic were published. On the Jewish side D. Honigmann: "The Reformation and the Jews," Breslau 1844; then on the Lutheran side Ernst Wilhelm Hengstenberg: "The Jews and the Christian church," 1857 (first published in the "Evangelische Kirchenzeitung," published as a book in 1859). Today Fischer's and Honigmann's writings are no longer extant.[77] Only Hengstenberg's work is accessible.[78] Apart from holding the academic office of professor of theology in Berlin, Hengstenberg was for more than 40 years editor of the "Evangelische Kirchenzeitung," the most influential church periodical of the 19th century. What Hengstenberg wrote in the "Evangelische Kirchenzeitung" on Luther's attitude as regards the Jews, and what he repeated in a book two years later, can be considered as the determining factor in forming the opinion of wide sections of German Protestantism. It is, by the way, possible that Hengstenberg's reflections on the relation of church and Jews were caused by a resolution of the Lutheran synod of Missouri, Ohio and other states. A year before, in 1856, these synods, quoting Luther for support, had renounced Chiliasm and had also abandoned the hope that a conversion of Israel was still possible. Hengstenberg warns against an overestimation of Luther's authority and regards it as fitting to make Luther's writings on the Jews the object of a careful study.[79]

Without approving of Chiliasm and clearly opposing the kind of passionate enthusiasm for Israel which made its way into Germany from England and Scotland, Hengstenberg followed the argumentation of Luther's treatise "That Jesus Christ Was Born a Jew," and quoted long passages from it.[80] The "spirit of a heartfelt love of the Jews"[81] is, according to Hengstenberg, the most essential thing to be learned from Luther. The completely different attitude of the aged Luther was presented by Hengstenberg through the use of quotations from "On the *Schem Hamphoras*," "On the Jews and their Lies," from the "Table Talks," and from the last warning against the Jews in Eisleben. Hengstenberg's comment on the aged Luther is very clear and leaves no doubt:

> This attitude toward the Jews which Luther had late in life is certainly very appropriate to make clear to us the difference between him and the apostles and to show how dubious it would be to follow such a master wholeheartedly without examining the Scriptures, a mistake the Lutheran Church has never made.[82]

Thus Hengstenberg, the first Lutheran theologian of the 19th century to deal with Luther's attitude as regards Jews, does not abstain from criticism. That the Lutheran Church was never to follow the late Luther seemed to be disproved 20 years later by the argumentation of the anti-Semitic Lutheran preacher at court, Adolf Stoecker. But Stoecker, a disciple of Hengstenberg, never quoted Luther's treatises on the Jews in his anti-Jewish speeches and papers. Whether or not he knew them, we do not know.[83] As the work of Johannes Brosseder reveals, there is no passage of Stoecker's where he refers to Luther's comments on the Jews. Therefore Stoecker's anti-Jewish agitations cannot be brought into connection with Luther's writings on the Jews.[84] In 1892 Friedrich Lezius, a Lutheran theologian from Dorpat and later professor in Konigsberg, was in the position to affirm with justification Hengstenberg's assessment in an even more salient form. In his study "Luther's attitude as regards the Jews"[85] Lezius praises the fact that Luther in 1523 had put an end to the medieval antagonism toward Jews, but he strongly condemns Luther's relapse into the medieval hatred of Jews at the end of his life. The well-known "Suggestions" to the princes written in 1543 Lezius called "scandalous measures, clearly contrary to the spirit of the Gospel."[86] Lezius reaches the following conclusive opinion: "It is obvious that Luther does not argue in accordance with the spirit of the New Testament and the Reformation. . . . The Protestant Church has therefore rejected the errors of the aging reformer as not binding for the church and only regards Luther's treatise "That Jesus

Christ Was Born a Jew," which was published in 1523, as the true expression of the spirit of the Reformation."[87] And a few lines further on: "The German nation did not want to follow . . . Luther's suggestions because they do not agree with the Gospel and the concepts of modern humanitarianism. . . . It was therefore beneficial to Christendom to ignore the admonitions of the mighty man."[88] As late as the end of the 19th century, therefore, it was possible for a Lutheran theologian to give such an opinion on the aged Luther's writings on the Jews. That Lezius was not an outsider can be seen in the standard theological work of German Protestantism before World War I, the "Encyclopedia of the Protestant Church and Theology." Here, as well, Luther's suggestions on how to deal with the Jewish question were, if mentioned at all, reported only with evident disagreement.[89]

Whenever people in the second half of the 19th century quote Luther in support of the struggle against the Jews, they are not Lutheran theologians. Luther's "Suggestions" to the princes are published in the catechism of anti-Semitism by Theodor Fritsch, the founder of "practical anti-Semitism."[90] Catholic anti-Semites like Georg Rosel referred to Luther in order to defeat the argument that "today's anti-Jewish movement was a relapse into medieval times and an affront to the achievements of the Reformation."[91] Within German Protestantism of the 19th century, however, there is practically nobody of any importance within Lutheran theology and church who referred to Luther to support an anti-Jewish position. Reinhold Lewin, the later Rabbi of Breslau, who in 1911 wrote his book "Luther's Position with Regard to the Jews" was awarded the annual prize of the Breslau Faculty of Protestant Theology for this work.[92] It appeared in the series "New Studies on the History of Theology and the Church" which was published by the renowned Lutheran theologians Nathanael Bonwetsch and Reinhold Seeberg. Lewin would hardly have thought it possible that Lutheran theologians would one day refer to Luther in order to legitimize the racial struggle against the Jews. But that this did happen in the 20th century, and to such a terrifying extent,[93] is no doubt the worst chapter of all in the reception of Luther. Writing this chapter, however, was not part of my task.

Professor Dr. Johannes Wallmann
Buchenwag 2
D-5810 Witten–Buchholz

Notes

1. Alex Bein, *Die Judenfrage. Biographie eines Weltproblems*, Vol. I, Stuttgart 1980, pp. 130 f. Quotation translated.
2. A. Bein, op. cit. Vol. II, 1980, p. 65. Quotation translated.
3. Johannes Brosseder, "Luthers Stellung zu den Juden im Spiegel seiner Interpreten. Interpretation und Rezeption von Luthers Schriften und Äusserungen zum Judentum im 19. und 20. Jahrhundert vor allem im deutschsprachigen Raum," Beiträge zur ökumenischen Theologie 8, München 1972.
4. G. Philipp, "Zinzendorf als Wegbereiter eines deutschen Philosemitismus," *Emuna* VII, 1972, p. 16.
5. C. Malitius, "Luther und die Juden," in: *Der Stürmer*, 11. Jahrgang, Nr. 46, November 1933, p. 4 (See Brosseder op. cit. pp. 184 f.) Quotation translated.
6. W. Linden, *Luthers Kampfschriften gegen das Judentum*, Berlin 1936, p. 46 (See Brosseder op. cit. p. 178). Quotation translated.
7. E.V. von Rudolf, *Dr. Martin Luther wider die Jüden. Vierhundert Jahre deutschen Ringens gegen jüdische Fremdherrschaft*, München 1940, p. 8 Quotation translated. E.V. von Rudolf is pseudonym for Rudolf von Elmayer–Vestenbrugg. For Elmayer–Vestenbrugg see Brosseder, op. cit. pp. 169 f.
8. Haim Hillel Ben Sasson, *Geschichte des Jüdischen Volkes*, Vol. II, München 1979, p. 323. Quotation translated.
9. Reinhold Lewin, "Luthers Stellung zu den Juden. Ein Beitrag zur Geschichte der Juden in Deutschland während des Reformationszeitalters." *Neue Studien zur Geschichte der Theologie und der Kirche*, hg. N. Bonwetsch und R. Seeberg, Nr. 10, Berlin 1911 (Reprint Aalen 1973), pp. 97 ff.
10. Lewin op. cit. p. 100.
11. *WA BR* 8, Nr. 3157, pp. 89-91. The letter is dated 11 June 1537. Cf. Eric W. Gritsch, *Martin—God's Court Jester*. Luther in Retrospect, Philadelphia 1983, p. 135.
12. Leaving aside the Formula of Concord, which dates from the post-Reformation era (1577) the classic books of the Lutheran confessions were written as follows: Luther's Small and Large Catechisms in 1529, Melanchthon's Augsburg Confession and Apology of the Augsburg Confession in 1530/31, Luther's Smalcald Articles in December 1536.
13. J. Cochlaeus, *Dialogue de bello contra Turcas in Anti-logias Lutheri*, 1529. See Rudolf Mau, "Luthers Stellung zu den Türken," in: Helmar Junghans (ed.), Leben und Werk Martin Luthers von *1526 bis 1546*, Berlin 1983, Vol. I., pp. 647-662; Vol. II, pp. 956-966.
14. The most famous remark in "An den christlichen Adel deutscher Nation" (To the Christian Nobility of the German Nation): "man sagt / das kein feyner weltlich regiment yrgend sey / dan bey dem Turcken / der doch wider geystlich noch weltlich recht hat / Bondern allein seinen Alkoran" (*WA* 6, 459, 23 ff.).
15. Luther, "Vom Kriege wider die Türken," 1529 (*WA* 30 II, 107-148); "Eine Heerpredigt wider den Türken," 1529 (*WA* 30 II, 160-197).
16. See Augsburg Confession Article I De Deo: "Damant . . . Mahometistas" (Die Bekenntnisschriften der evangelisch–lutherischen Kirche, Göttingen 1979,[8] p. 51).
17. The notion of the "double Antichrist", the Pope as the western Antichrist and Mohammed of the Turk as the eastern Antichrist, is more due to Melanchthon than to Luther. It appears in Melanchthon's Apology of the Augsburg Confession Article XV (*Die Bekenntnisschriften der evangelisch–lutherischen Kirche*, p. 300). For the doctrine of the

"double Antichrist" as the opinio communis of older Lutheran theology see Gottfried Seebass, Article "Antichrist" in Theologische Realenzyklopadie, Vol. III, Berlin–New York 1978, pp. 28 ff. (especially p. 33).

18. Cf. note 24 below.

19. Luther wrote this hymn in 1541 as "Ein Kinderlied, zu singen, wider die zween Erzfeinde Christi und seiner heiligen Kirche, den Papst und den Türken" (WA 35, 467 f.). As early as 1548, after the defeat of the Lutherans in the Smalcaldic war, the Lutherans were compelled to change the verse in "Und wehr des Satans List und Mord," but afterwards used the original words until the end of the 17th century.

20. See the different portrayals of the Moslems and the Jews in comparison with the Christians given by Christian Scriver, Seelen–Schatz (1675), Magdeburg und Leipzig 1727, Vol. I, pp. 455 ff. The Moslems are here characterized as bound by the devil, whereas the Jews are only bound by blindness. Also Johann Arndt's "Four Books of True Christianity" (1605–10), the most popular of the devotional books of older Lutheranism, which have been published in innumerable editions throughout the century do not contain any passages, that could be called "anti-Jewish." On the other hand Arndt offers a prayer against the Turks, referring to the blasphemies of those enemies of Christendom (J. Arndt, Paradiesgartlein, part IV, prayer 34). One has, of course, to consider, that the Reformation period and the period of the so-called Lutheran Orthodoxy coincides with the period of the "Türkengefahr" (Turkish danger), which lasted from the early 16th century until the end of the seventeenth century (Liberation of Vienna 1683).

21. Georg Nigrinus, Jüden Feind. Von den Edelen Früchten der Thalmudischen Jüden / so jetziger Zeit in Teuschlands wonen / eine ernste / Thalmudischen Jüden / so jetziger Zeit in Teuschlands wonen / eine ernste / wolgegründe Schrifft / Darin kurtzlich angezeiget wird / Das sie die gröste Lesterer vnd Verechter vnsers Herrn Jesu Christi / Darzu abgesagte vnd vnversünliche Feinde der Christen sind. Dargegen Freunde vnd Verwande der Türcken. . . . Derhalben sie billich von einer jeden Christlichen Oberkeit nicht geduldet werden solten / oder dermassen gehalten / wie jn Gott selbs / die Weltlichen vnd Geistliche Recht aufferleget. . . . , Oberursel (Nicolaus Henricus) 1570. 8⁰. (112 Bl.).

22. Nicolaus Selnecker, Von den Jüden vnd jren Lügen. Vom Schem Hamphoras der Jüden / vnd vom Geschlecht Christi. Wider die Sabbather / vnd der Jüden Lügen vnd betrug. Durch D. Martinum Lutherum. Item / Von den teglichen Gottslesterungen der Jüden wider vnsern HERRN Jhesum Christum / wider vnsere liebe Obrigkeit / vnd wider alle Christen. Alles jetzt auff ein newes fromen rechten Christen . . . mitgetheilet, Leipzig (Jacob Berwald) 1577. 12⁰. (392 Bl.). Vorh. Herzog August Bibliothek Wolfenbuttel: Alvensleben Ba 109. Another copy of that book in UB Leipzig: St. Thomas 1286 (I owe this knowledge to Dr. Ernst Koch, Leipzig). Selnecker's book was not available to Lewin (see op. cit. p. X) or to Brosseder (see op. cit. p. 46 n. 13). So recently the existence of that book has been problematized (H. Grote, "Luther und die Juden." Materialdienst des Konfessionskundlichen Instituts Bensheim 34, 1983, p. 64).

23. Op. cit. preface.

24. The original German version "wie an den Juden zu sehen" was translated "ut est videre in obstinatis et perditissimis hominibus, Judaeis" (Die Bekenntnisschriften der evangelisch-lutherischen Kirche, p. 1080).

25. S. Kracauer, Geschichte der Juden von Frankfurt am Main, I, pp. 129 f. Kracauer mentions two edicts of Emperor Rudolf II (dating Prag 10.7.1595 and Speyer 7.9.1595) against that "famos libell so wider die Jüdischeit ausgegangen." According to Kracauer the book was entitled D. Martini Luther Christlicher Unterricht von der Jüden Lügen wider die Person unseres Herrn Jesu Christi. A copy of that book is not known.

26. *Tractat Von den Jüden und jhren Lügen.* . . . Zum andernmahl zu Wittenberg gedruckt: Jetzo aber widerumb auff erhalter guthertziger frommer Christen auffs neuere übersehen / vnd zu treuherziger Christlicher Erinnerung aller vnd jeder Obrigkeit/ so Jüden vnter sich wohnen haben / die abzuschaffen, Frankfurt a.m. (Johann Sauren) 1613. Cf. *WA* 53, p. 415. The treatise with this title and year of appearance forms the second part of the following printing: *Drey Christliche / in Gottes Wort wolgegründete Tractat.* Der Erste Von dem hohen vermeynten Jüdischen Geheymnuss / dem Schem Hamphoras / . . . Der Ander Von dem Geschlecht Christi . . . Der Dritte Von den Juden vnd ihren Lugen. . . . Frankfurt a. M. (Gottfr. Tampach) 1617. 40. 92 + 168 pp. Extant Herzog August Bibliothek Wolfenbüttel 189 Th (6).

27. Cf. Simon Dubnow, *Weltgeschichte des jüdischen Volkes,* Vol. VI, Die Neuzeit. Erste Periode, Berlin 1927, pp. 234 ff.

28. Useful is: Julius Fürst, *Bibliotheca Judaica.* Bibliographisches Handbuch umfassend die Druckwerke der judischen Literatur einschliesslich der über Juden und Judenthum veröffentlichten Schriften nach alphabetischer Ordnung der Verfasser bearbeitet, Vol. I–III, Leipzig 1863 (Reprint Hildesheim 1960); Joh. Christoph Wolf, *Bibliotheca Hebraea, sive Notitia tum Auctorum Hebr. cujuscunque aetatis, tum Scriptorum, quae vel Hebraice primum exarata vel ab aliis conversa sunt,* Vol. I–IV, Hamburg u. Leipzig 1715–33. For our purpose: Vol. II: *Bibliotheca Hebraea Pars II.* Quae praeter Historiam Scripturae sacrae. . . . Bibliothecam Iudicam et Antijudaicam aperit, Hamburg 1721.

29. Anthonius Margaritha, *Der gantz Jüdisch glaub mit sampt ainer grundtlichen vnd warhafften anzaygunge /* Aller Satzungen / Ceremonien / Gebetten / Haymliche vnd offentliche Gebreuch/ deren sich die Juden halten / durch das gantz Jar, Augsburg 1530. Second edition Leipzig 1531. For Margaritha's influence on Luther's "On the Jews and their Lies" see WA 53, p. 413 and especially Walther Bienerth, *Martin Luther und die Juden, Ein Quellenbuch,* Frankfurt a.M. 1982, pp. 135-137.

30. The different editions were listed by Reineccius in his preface to the edition Leipzig 1705.

31. Ernst Ferdinand Hess, *Juden Geissel / Das ist: Ein Newe sehr nütze vnd gründtliche Erweisung / das Jhesus Christus / Gottes vnd der heiligen Jungfrauwen Marien Sohn / der wahre verheissene vnd gesandte Messias sey. Wider alle noch jetziger zeit verstockte vnd verfluchte Jüden* . . . Fritzlar 1598. Ernst Ferdinand Hess was a Jewish physician, who converted circa 1582 to Roman Catholic faith and dedicated his book to the Archbishop of Mainz. Hess's *Judengeissel* was reprinted often: Erfurt 1599. 1600. 1602. 1605; Strassburg 1601. 1605; Paderborn 1606. Cf. Wolf, Bibliotheca Hebraea, Vol. I, p. 138; Vol. II, p. 1006.

32. Ernst Ferdinand Hess *Speculum Judaeorum. Das ist / Juden Spiegel. Ein New sehr nützlich Büchlein / darin sich nicht allein die gottlose lästerer / schänder / schmäher Göttlichen Worts / die Juden in besehen* . . . Erfurt 1602.

33. Samuel Friedrich Brentz, *Jüdischer abgestreifter Schlangenbalg. Das ist:* Grundtliche Entdeckung vnd Verwerffung aller lasterung vnd Lugen / derer sich das gifftige Judische Schlangengeziefer vnnd Otterngezicht / wider den frombsten/ vnschuldigen Juden Christum Jesum . . . theils in den verfluchten Synagogen/ theils in Hausern vnd heimlichen zusammenkunfften pflegt zugebrauchen, Augsburg 1614. Brentz, baptized at Feuchtwangen in 1601 (southern Germany), mentions Luther's friendly attitude towards the Jews and how Luther later on changed his mind in "On the Jews and Their Lies." Brentz does not cite Luther's anti-Jewish writings, but apparently he is influenced by them (cf. the title of his book). From the Jewish side Brentz was attacked by Rabbi Salman Zewi,

Jüdischer Theriack, Hanau 1615. A reprint of Zewi's book in 1680 was answered by the Nürnberg Pastor Johann Wülffer, *Theriaca Judaica ad examen revocata*, Altdorf 1681.

34. Christian Gerson, *Der Jüden Thalmud Furnembster innhalt / vnd Widerlegung*, Goslar 1607. Further editions: Gera 1613, 1618, Erfurt 1659, Leipzig 1685, 1698. Christian Gerson was born at Recklinghausen in 1569, was baptized at Halberstadt in 1600 and died as a pastor at Dröbel near Bernburg/Anhalt in 1627. Gerson speaks in favor of tolerance concerning the Jews and finds support for his friendly attitude towards the Jews in Luther's writing "That Jesus Christ was born a Jew": "In Betrachtung das auch D. Luther schreibet darumb / wer meine bitte / das man säuberlich mit ihnen umbginge / vnd aus der Schrifft sie vnterrichtete . . . das man sie gleich für Hunde hält / was sollten wir Guts an ihnen schaffen? Item / das man ihnen verbeut / unter uns zu arbeiten / handtieren / und andere Menschlich Gemeinschafft haben / damit man sie zu wuchern treibt. Zu welchem Ende auch ich dieses Büchlein geschrieben . . ." (Epistola Dedicatoria Bl. b IV v). It is most likely, that Gerson, who wrote the dedication to his book 24 June 1607, had a knowledge of Ernst Ferdinand Hess *Juden Geissel*, which had been published very often the years before (cf. Note 31). So Luther serves as an authority for Christian tolerance toward the Jews against Christian intolerance. Christian Gerson was highly estimated in the Lutheran tradition. Cf. Christian Scriver, *Seelen–Schatz*, Vol. I, pp. 135 f.; J.F.A. de le Roi, *Die evangelische Christenheit und die Juden*, Vol. I, Karlsruhe u. Leipzig 1884 (Reprint Leipzig 1974), pp. 117-122.

35. Johann Andreas Eisenmenger, *Entdecktes Judenthum / Oder Gründlicher und Warhaffter Bericht / Welchergestalt Die verstockte Juden die Hochheilige Drey–Einigkeit . . . erschrecklicher Weise lästern und verunehren / die Heil. Mutter Christi verschmähen / das Neue Testament / . . . spöttisch durchziehen / und die gantze Christenheit auff das äusserste verachten und verfluchen . . . Alles aus ihren eignen / und zwar sehr vielen mit grosser Mühe . . . durchlesenen Büchern . . . erwiesen*, I–II Königsberg (richtig: Berlin) 1711. 4⁰.

36. Cf. Bein, *Die Judenfrage*, Vol. I, pp. 170 ff.

37. Joh. Andr. Eisenmenger's . . . *Entdecktes Judentum* . . . Zeitgemäss überarbeitet und herausgegeben von Franz Xaver Schieferl, Dresden 1893.

38. Cf. G. Dalman, "Eisenmenger, Johann Andreas" in: *Realencyklopädie für protestantische Theologie und Kirche*, 3. edition, Vol. V, pp. 276 f. Jewish Encycl. V, pp. 80 ff.; The Universal Jewish Encycl. IV, p. 36 f.; Brosseder (see note 3) pp. 82 f.

39. E.g. Philipp von Limborch and Johann Buxtorf.

40. Eisenmenger, *Entdecktes Judentum*, Vol. I, p. 506.

41. Cf. Wolfgang Franzius, *Schola Sacrificiorum Patriarchalicum sacra . . . per Disputationes XX*, Wittenberg 1616. Disputatio X and XI contains a report on a Wittenberg disputation between Franzius and a learned Jew, who on his way from Italy to Hamburg visited Wittenberg University.

42. See Bossert, "Osiander, Lukas I.", *Realencyklopädie für protestantische Theologie und Kirche*, Vol. XIV, 1904, p. 310, 16 ff. Osiander's protest against Duke Friedrich I of Württemberg dated 13th March 1598 is published in: *Württembergische Landtagsakten* II, 1, Stuttgart 1910, pp. 498 ff.

43. Protest of the Lutheran ministry of the city Braunschweig dated 13th November 1578. Herzog August Bibliothek Wolfenbüttel Cod. Guelf. 14.6. Aug Bl. 223-228.

44. The opinions were published some years later by Georg Dedekenn, *Thesauri Consiliorum et Decisionum Volumen I Ecclesiastica continens. Das ist: Vornehmer Vniversitäten hochlöblicher Collegien/ wolbestallter Consistorien/ auch sonst hochgelährter Theologen und Juristen Rath, Bedencken, Antwort, Belehrung, Erkentnuss, Bescheide vnd Urtheile*

... Hamburg 1623, pp. 139-146 (Jena opinion dated 13. September 1611), pp. 146-149 (Frankfurt opinion). Cf. Simon Dubnow, op. cit. (see note 27) pp. 248 ff.

45. Op. cit. pp. 141 f.

46. Op. cit. p. 142: "In Betrachtung nun dieser Vrsachen / halten wir einhellig dafür / dass in Rebus p(ublicis) et urbibus Christianorum die Jüden auff gewisse mass wol konnen tolerirt vnd geduldet werden."

47. Johann Gerhard, *Loci theologici*, Vol. VI, Jena 1619. The question "An tolerandi in Republica Judaei" is treated by Gerhard in Locus XXVII De Magistratu Politico, pp. 890-900.

48. Johannes Müller, *Judaismus oder Judenthumb* / Das ist Ausführlicher Bericht von des Jüdischen Volckes Vnglauben / Blindheit vnd Verstockung ... Zu befestigung vnsers Christlichen Glaubens / Hintertreibung der Jüdischen Lästerung / auch nohtwendigen Vnterricht derer Christen / die täglich mit Jüden vmbgehen, Hamburg 1644. 1490 pp.

49. For instance the question, whether religious books of the Jews should be burned, is explicitly denied by Müller.

50. For a just evaluation of Johannes Müller, who is often called a narrow-minded Lutheran zealot, see Gerhard Müller, "Christlich–Jüdisches Religionsgespräch im Zeitalter der Protestantischen Orthodoxie. Die Auseinandersetzung Johann Müller mit Rabbi Isaak Trokis 'Hizzuk Emuna,' " in: Glaube, Geist, Geschichte. Festschrift für Ernst Benz, ed. G. Müller and W. Zeller, Leiden 1967, pp. 513-524.

51. W. Güde, *Die rechtliche Stellung der Juden in den Schriften deutscher Juristen des 16. und 17. Jahrhunderts*, Sigmaringen 1981, p. 21: "In der zeitgenössischen theologischen Literatur wird denn auch weitgehend die Meinung vertreten, dass man die Juden, ohne zu sündigen, nicht dulden dürfe."

52. *Denkwürdigkeiten der Glückel von Hameln.* Aus dem Jüdisch–Deutschen übersetzt von Alfred Feilchenfeld, Darmstadt 1979 (Reprint of 4. edition Berlin 1923).

53. Cf. Johannes Wallmann, *Philipp Jakob Spener und die Anfänge des Pietismus*, Tübingen 1970, pp. 240 ff.

54. "Und wie unser lieber Lutherus darvor hielte / wir solten alle Juden umb dess einigen Juden Jesu willen lieben / so sollen wir auch ihr gantzes geschlecht umb dieses einigen alleredelsten Juden Jesu willen hochachten" (Funeral Sermon on Georg Philipp Liechtstein 10 February 1682, in: Ph.J. Spener, *Christliche Leichpredigten*, Vol. II, Frankfurt a.M. 1685, p. 257.

55. "Ist ein einiger Jude, um deswillen (schreibt D. Luther an den Juden Josel) sol man alle Juden liebe haben" (*Sonderbare Gespräche zwischen einem Reisenden und Allerhand anderen Personen von Allerley in der Religion vorkommenden Wahrheiten*, Altona 1739,[2] p. 106. Reprint in: Nikolaus Ludwig von Zinzendorf, *Hauptschriften*, ed. Erich Beyreuther and Gerhard Meyer, Vol. I, Hildesheim 1962.

56. G. Arnold, *Unparteiische Kirchen-und Ketzerhistorie*, Part II, Book XVI, Chapt. 34, Paragraph 19 ff. (Edition Frankfurt a.M. 1700, Vol. II, pp. 405 f.).

57. J.G. Walch, *Martin Luthers Sämtliche Schriften*, Vol. XX, Halle a.S. 1747, p. 91.

58. Erdmann Neumeister, *Priesterliche Lippen in Bewahrung der Lehre*, Görlitz 1714, pp. 1797 ff.

59. "Juden, oder Jüden" in: *Johann Heinrich Zedlers Grosses Vollständiges Universal Lexikon*, Vol. XIV, 1735, pp. 1497 ff. (Reprint Graz 1961). Cf. Barbara Suchy, *Lexikographie und Juden im 18. Jahrhundert.* Die Darstellung von Juden und Judentum in den englischen, französischen und deutschen Lexika und Enzyklopädien im Zeitalter der Aufklärung, Köln–Wien 1979, p. 239: "Das, was 14. Band, der 1735 erschien, auf 11 Seiten unter dem Stichwort 'Juden' steht, ist wohl einzigartig in seiner Art. Der Artikel mutet

Notes

an wie eine Hetzpredigt eines zu einem Kreuzzug aufrufenden mittelalterlichen, religiösen Eiferers." The fact that those passages containing the wildest accusations against the Jews are quotations from Erdmann Neumeister, is not mentioned by Barbara Suchy.

60. See op. cit. p. 1502.

61. S.J. Baumgarten, *Theologisches Bedenken von gewissenhafter Duldung der Juden und ihres Gottesdienstes unter den Christen, Halle*, p. 1745.

62. See op. cit. p. 9.

63. J.S. Semler, *Beantwortung der Fragmente eines Ungenannten, Halle*, 1779, p. 325.

64. Ibid.

65. See S.J. Baumgarten, *Geschichte der Religionsparteien*, ed. J.S. Semler, Halle, p. 1766 (Reprint Hildesheim 1966), pp. 257-340 ("Von den Juden") and pp. 340-366 ("Von jüdischen Schriften").

66. S. Ascher, *Eisenmenger der Zweite*. Nebst einem vorangesetzten Sendschreiben an Herrn Professor Fichte in Jena, Berlin 1794. For the complex problem of Fichte's attitude toward the Jews see A. Bein, op. cit., Vol. II, pp. 194 f.

67. J.G. Hamann, Golgatha und Scheblimini, 1784 (= Sämtliche Werke ed. J. Nadler, Vol. III, Wien 1951).

68. See A. Bein op. cit. Vol. II, p. 120. Johann Gottfried Herder, who had a thorough knowledge of Luther's writings, commented often upon the Jews. Though his comments were not always positive, the result of the bulk of them was that even in the nineteenth century he was proclaimed by the anti-Semites to be an enemy, and by the Jews themselves to be a friend. There is only one passage, in his *Adrastea*, in which Herder mentions Luther in connection with the Jews, specifically, Luther's opinion that the Jews could not be converted, which, says Herder, Luther expressed "too harshly," in the manner of his time. (J.G. Herder, *Sämtliche Werke*, ed. B. Suphan, Vol. XXIV, Berlin 1886, p. 62).

69. C.W.F. Grattenauer, *Wider die Juden. Ein Wort der Warnung an alle unser christliche Mitbuřger*. Berlin 1803 (six editions within the year 1803!). Grattenauer doesn't refer to Luther, but to Voltaire: "Voltaire war der letzte, der die Juden in Berlin von dieser Seite richtig kannte und schilderte" (Grattenauer, *Erster Nachtrag zu seiner Erklarung über seine Schrift: Wider die Juden*. Berlin 1803, p. 75).

70. J.J. Fries, *Über die Gefährdung des Wohlstands und Charakters der Deutschen durch die Juden*, Heidelberg 1816.

71. Ascher even criticizes that Luther's name had been used in the invitations, when later during the "Feier" anti-Jewish events occurred. Cf. S. Ascher, *Die Wartburgfeier mit Hinsicht auf Deutschlands religiöse und politische Stimmung*, Leipzig 1818.

72. Cf. G. Ott, *Ernst Moritz Arndt*, Bonn 1966, p. 179 note 43.

73. For Ranke and his fundamental influence on Luther research in the 19th century cf. H. Bornkamm, *Luther im Spiegel der deutschen Geistesgeschichte*, Göttingen 1970², pp. 41 ff.

74. After having finished my paper the following writings came to my knowledge: E.C. Kruse, "Luther und die Juden," in: *Kieler Blätter*, herausgegeben von einer Gesellschaft Kieler Professoren; Vol. II, Kiel 1819, pp. 337-389 (followed by notes of Twesten pp. 389-394); (Anonymous), "Luthers und v. Herders Stimmen über die Juden." Nebst einem Epilog. Deutschland, 1817. The latter, a pamphlet published in Lübeck, is anti-Semitic and claims, that Arndt, Rühs, and Fries in their struggle against the Jews could have referred to Luther (which, according to the anonymous author, they obviously had not known). The article, written by Kruse, a Lutheran pastor, is in the contrary very

critical against Luther's suggestions to the princes: "Sie sind unmenschlich und zweck-widrig zugleich" (p. 385). Evidently, both papers did not reach a wider public.
75. Dr. Martin Luther's sämmtliche Werke, Vol. 32, Erlangen 1832.
76. Ludwig Fischer, *Dr. Martin Luther von den Jüden und ihren Lügen. Ein crystallisirter Auszug aus dessen Schriften über der Juden Verblendung, Jammer, Bekehrung und Zukunft. Ein Beitrag zur Charakteristik dieses Volkes*, Leipzig 1838.
77. See Brosseder op. cit. p. 41 n 4. In the meantime, after having finished my paper, I found a copy in the Municipal Library Braunschweig. Fischer's book is a polemic against the emancipation of the Jews, in particular against the literati of the "young Germany" (das junge Deutschland), i.e., Ludwig Börne, and above all, Heinrich Heine. Confronted with an enthusiastic, even worshipful attitude toward Luther among emancipated German Jews, the author wants to remind his readers of how Luther judged the Jews. Fischer does not share Luther's pessimism about the possibility of a conversion of the Jews. And he also explicitly states just at the beginning that "in our days of tolerance and eman-cipation we cannot adopt the fanaticism (Eifer) of Luther" (p. 3 f.). He does not cite Luther's recommendations on the burning of the synagogues, but is quoting extensive theological passages from different writings of Luther, dealing more with Luther's struggle against glorification of reason than against the Jews. So the title of Fischer's book is misleading. Fischer was answered in *Allgemeine Zeitung des Judenthums* by an anonymous Jewish author, who claimed "dass, wenn wir von Luther's Wesen die gedachte Verfah-rensweise gegen die Juden abziehen, dennoch der grösse Genius übrig bleibt, und wir abgesehen von diesem einzelnen Punkte, an früherer Hochachtung und Bewunderung seiner noch nicht einen Deut abzuziehen brauchen . . ." (*Allgemeine Zeitung des Ju-denthums*, 2. Jahrgang, Leipzig 1838, No. 71, p. 279).
78. E. W. Hengstenberg, "Die Juden und die christliche Kirche," in: *Evangelische Kir-chenzeitung* 60, Berlin 1857, 449-459; 497-504; 505-520; 652-662; 665-667; 673-680. A second edition published in bookform: E.W. Hengstenberg, *Die Opfer der Heiligen Schrift. Die Juden und die christliche Kirche*, Berlin 1859. I am citing the second edition.
79. See Hengstenberg p. 63. I was not able to verify Hengstenberg's statements.
80. Op. cit. pp. 52 ff.
81. Op. cit. p. 54.
82. "Diese Stellung, die Luther in seinen späteren Jahren zu den Juden einnahm, ist allerdings recht geeignet, uns den Unterschied zwischen ihm und den Aposteln zur Anschauung zu bringen und uns zu zeigen, wie bedenklich es wäre, sich einem solchen Meister unbedingt und ohne Prüfung nach der Schrift hinzugeben, was auch die Lutherische Kirche nie gethan hat" (op. cit. p. 57).
83. According to Uriel Tal (*Christians and the Jews in Germany. Religion, Politics, and Ideology in the Second Reich, 1870–1914*, Ithaca and London 1975) the parallel between Luther's "Von den Jüden und ihren Lügen" and Stöcker was pointed out by an otherwise unknown Pfarrgehilfe A. Freilich in a meeting in 1879 (op. cit. p. 258 n. 52).
84. On Stöcker see Brosseder, op. cit. pp. 74 ff. n. 16.
85. F. Lezius, "Luthers Stellung zu den Juden." *Baltische Monatsschrift* 39, Riga 1892, pp. 336-345. For a detailed analysis of this article see Brosseder op. cit. pp. 68 ff.
86. Op. cit. p. 314 ("Diese ungeheuerlichern, dem Geiste des Evangeliums schnurstracks engegen laufenden Massregeln . . .").
87. "Es liegt auf der Hand, dass Luther hier nicht aus dem Geist des neuen Testaments und der Reformation heraus argumentiert. . . . Die evangelische Kirche hat daher die Irrtümer des alternden Reformators als für sich nicht massgebend abgelehnt und sieht in der Schrift

Notes

Luthers, dass Jesus Christus ein geborener Jude sei, welche 1523 erschien, den wahren Ausdruck reformatorischen Geistes" (op. cit. pp. 344 f.).

88. "Diese Ratschläge Luthers . . . hat das deutsche Volk nicht befolgen wollen, weil sie mit dem Evangelium und den Begriffen moderner Humanität sich nicht vertragen. . . . Es hat die Christenheit daher wohlgethan, diese Ermahnungen des gewaltigen Mannes unbeachtet zu lassen" (op. cit. p. 345).

89. Realenzyklopädie für protentantische Theologie und Kirche, 3. edition, 1896-1913. Luther's attitude toward the Jews is treated by K.F. Heman in the article "Israel, Geschichte, nachbiblische" (Vol. 9, p. 505, 35 ff.) and "Mission unter den Juden" (Vol. 13, p. 177, 13 ff.).

90. Th. Fritsch, Handbuch der Judenfrage, 30. edition, Leipzig 1931 (Antisemiten–Katechismus, Leipzig 1887). See Brosseder op. cit. p. 100.

91. G. Rösel, Luther und die Juden. Ein Beitrag zu der Frage: 'Hat die Reformation gegen Juda Toleranz geübt?', Münster/W. 1893. See Brosseder op. cit. pp. 85 ff.

92. Cf. Guido Kisch, "Necrologue Reinhold Lewin 1888–1942," in: Historia Judaica 8, 1946, pp. 217-219.

93. Cf. The pamphlet of the Lutheran bishop of Thuringia Martin Sasse, a member of the "Deutsche Christen": "Martin Luther über die Juden: Weg mit ihnen!," Freiburg/ Br. 1938. See Brosseder op. cit. pp. 208 f. One has, of course, to recognize, that the misuse of Luther's writings against the Jews for the purpose of racial antisemitism originated after World War I not in Lutheran theology, but against Lutheran theology in the "völkische Bewegung". Cf. Alfred Falb, Luther und die Juden (= Deutschlands führende Männer und das Judentum, Vol. 4), München 1921. Falb, who plays a key role in the transmission of the knowledge about Luther's writings on the Jews to the "völkische Bewegung" (see Brosseder passim), complains: "What have they (The theologians) made of our German prophet! They have suppressed his assessment of the dangers of Judaism, and withheld it from the German people" (p. 53). Those complaints are—with reference to Falb's book—repeated by Dietrich Eckart, the friend and teacher of Adolf Hitler, in his pamphlet "Der Bolschewismus von Moses bis Lenin. Zwiegespräch zwischen Adolf Hitler und mir" München 1924 (cf. p. 32: "Unseren Protestanten ist nicht mehr zu helfen . . . Luthers Geist . . . scheint bei ihnen ganz ausgespielt zu haben. In der Frage aller Fragen, der Juden-frage, schweigen sie ihn entweder tot oder suchen ihn zu 'mildern'.") This pamphlet is a study-work, not a protocol of a real dialogue. It is unlikely, that Hitler himself read the book by Falb and thus got a detailed knowledge of Luther's attitude toward the Jews. In Hitler's early speeches and writings no subject is treated as often as the Jewish question, but never is Luther mentioned in this context (cf. E. Jäckel—A. Kuhn, Hitler. Sämtliche Aufzeichnungen 1905-1924, Stuttgart 1980). The protestant church is praised in Hitler's main work Mein Kampf because of its engagement for the national question, but harshly criticized for favorizing the Jews (A. Hitler, Mein Kampf, München, 1930, p. 123).